THE ART OF MIXING DRINKS

THE ART OF MIXING DRINKS

by C. Carter Smith, Jr.

Introduction by Peter Kriendler

THE WARNER LIFESTYLE LIBRARY

WARNER BOOKS

A Warner Communications Company

THE WARNER LIFESTYLE LIBRARY

 Created by Media Projects Incorporated

Staff, Media Projects Incorporated
Carter Smith, President
Beverly Gary Kempton, Senior Editor
Susan Dempsey Brown, Contributing Editor
James E. Ramage, Designer
Ellen Coffey, Assistant Editor
Mary T. O'Connor, Consulting Editor

Cover photograph: Grey Advertising (Renfield Importers)
Title page photograph by Sally Andersen-Bruce
Back cover photographs: left, Joseph E. Seagram & Sons, Inc.; top right, Rums of Puerto Rico;
bottom right, iittala glassworks.

Warner Books, Inc., 75 Rockefeller Plaza, New York, N.Y. 10019

A Warner Communications Company

Printed in the United States of America
First Printing: May 1981
10 9 8 7 6 5 4 3 2 1

Library of Congress Cataloguing in Publication Data

Smith, C. Carter.
    The art of mixing drinks.

    (The Warner lifestyle library)
    Includes index.
    1. Cocktails.   2. Alcoholic beverages.   I. Title.
II. Series: Warner lifestyle library.
TX951.S59   641.8'74   80-39903
ISBN 0-446-51218-4 (hardcover)
ISBN 0-446-97759-4 (pbk. U.S.A.)
ISBN 0-446-97873-6 (pbk. Canada)

Also in the Warner Lifestyle Library
The Art of Gift Wrapping
The Art of Table Decoration
The Art of Flower Arranging

CONTENTS

INTRODUCTION

The principles of hospitality that have always guided the way we run our "21" Club are very much the same as those explained in this handsome book. After all, whether you are a restaurateur or a host in a private home, you want your guests to feel comfortable and to have a good time. People respond to thoughtfulness, and that is what entertaining is all about.

One way to achieve this is with the food and liquid refreshment you serve. That does not mean you must come forth with caviar, twenty-five-year-old Scotch, or $200-a-bottle champagne. It means that whatever you serve, simple or sumptuous, must show you care. If it is wine and cheese, the cheese should be served appetizingly; the wine, the best in its price range. There is a surprising difference in quality even among the many reasonably priced wines. It is your obligation to find the best one.

You should pay a great deal of attention to the way the food and drinks are presented. Remember, before we taste anything, we see it. Whether you are a professional restaurateur or the host or hostess at home, everything you serve should appeal to the eye. A summer drink in a tall glass garnished with fruit or sprig of mint is a cooling and appealing sight. Hors d'oeuvres served on interesting plates or garnished with parsley look more appetizing. It is the subtle touch that shows your concern.

Then there is that quality known as ambiance — the atmosphere you create for your guests. If you create one that makes your guests feel comfortable, they will enjoy themselves. I have often been told that the atmosphere at "21" is warm. Our regular patrons call our place their home away from home — and with good reason. Oak paneling, soft lighting, tables comfortably spaced, checkered tablecloths, waiters in red waistcoats, are all part of the warm atmosphere we wanted to provide, and it seems to have worked. Our ambiance, like our art collection, wasn't acquired overnight. Each step was carefully planned, and even today any change is made only after much thought and discussion.

In the home, too, as this book reveals, there are numerous ways to create an atmosphere and bring your own style to a party. Let your home be your signature and reflect who you are, no matter what kind of party you give. There is no reason why every cocktail or dinner party must be the same. Whether it is an informal gathering or a very formal party, the trick is to be yourself. Show your guests you are glad to have them there, and then prove it with what you serve and the way you serve it.

The Art of Mixing Drinks gives some valuable suggestions on how to entertain when drinks are being served. Carter Smith, the author of this book, told me he studied many bar guides and books on entertaining in order to discover the current state of the art. I believe that he did a fine job.

You will learn from this book. And you'll learn from experience. You will succeed if you give your guests the best you have — especially the best of yourself. That's hospitality.

Peter Kriendler
President of "21" Club, Inc.

PROVIDING IN STYLE

Entertaining today is very much an art, and its rules are those of comfort, courtesy, and hospitality. As the artist you must know about the basic materials and techniques, as well as how to plan and implement parties. You also want to create an atmosphere that reflects your special taste for your guests' special pleasure.

When planning a large party or a small get-together, attention to details can make all the difference. It is one of the highest compliments you can pay your guests. A full-bodied jug wine served in individual carafes can transform a simple spaghetti dinner into a special occasion because it shows your guests you really care.

A party is an occasion to bring out your best tableware and, better still, to stretch your imagination. Use those baskets you have been collecting to offer bread and crackers at a cocktail party, or build a fiesta around the attractive tequila glasses you purchased at the flea market last summer.

The spirit of friendship and hospitality is certainly embodied in your party plans, but providing the best of everything for your guests does not mean you have to spend extravagantly. You can express your good wishes by serving a favorite drink perfectly prepared to your guest's taste and presenting it in a beautiful glass.

The Art of Mixing Drinks has been designed to help you acquire some of the technical skills you will need to entertain with style — to mix and serve drinks with panache, to organize for company, to make your guests feel welcome in your home, and to enable you to enjoy their company.

Opposite: These elegant crystal decanters for whiskey, wine, and liqueurs embody the principle of providing in style.

YOUR HOME BAR

Any area in your home or apartment where you can mix a drink easily can be used as a bar. If you entertain frequently, yours may have its own built-in sink, refrigerator, and automatic icemaker. Or you can use an antique dry sink or a turn-of-the-century marble-topped washstand. Some hosts and hostesses have converted unused closets and pantries into bar areas, while others simply pour in the kitchen.

No matter how lavish or simple your bar, it should have a flat, uncluttered work surface, a shelf for glasses, a drawer or basket for tools, and storage space for wines and spirits.

The wines and spirits in your liquor cabinet will depend on your preferences and on those of your friends. A well-stocked bar differs from region to region and even from season to season. The following list offers suggestions for a basic bar stocked for imbibing before and after dinner. When you make *your* list, tailor it to suit your needs.

SPIRITS
- Scotch (one bottle light, one bottle heavy)
- bourbon or rye whiskey
- blended whiskey (for mixed drinks)
- Canadian or Irish whiskey (optional)
- vodka (American or Chinese for mixed drinks; Polish, Finnish, or Russian for drinking straight)
- rum (one bottle white, one bottle Jamaican)
- tequila
- brandy (use "starred" brandies for mixed drinks)

VERMOUTHS AND APERITIFS
- French dry vermouth
- Italian sweet vermouth
- aperitifs (Lillet, Dubonnet, Byrrh, or Pernod)
- Italian bitters (Campari or Punt e Mes)

A good dry vermouth should be light in color and subtle in taste; sweet vermouth should be sweet (with a bittersweet aftertaste) and never cloying. Both sweet and dry vermouth should be able to stand on their own when poured over ice. Dry vermouth is essential to the Martini (even if only a drop is used), and the Rob Roy and the Manhattan are made with sweet vermouth.

BEER AND WINE
- beer, stout, or ale (domestic or imported)
- dry white wine (six bottles)
- dry red wine (three bottles)

Always serve beer in sparkling clean glasses and never serve it too cold (it should be 45°–50°F. to bring out its full flavor). Take beer out of the refrigerator about fifteen minutes before you're ready to pour. Hold the can or bottle one or two inches above the rim of the glass and pour directly to the bottom to build a rich and creamy cap.

SHERRIES, BRANDIES, AND LIQUEURS
- dry sherry
- medium-dry sherry
- port or Madeira (a vintage bottle)
- cognac (a fine, old bottle for sipping only)
- fruit brandy
- liqueurs (three or four of your choice)

The differences between fruit brandies and liqueurs (cordials) often create confusion. Fruit brandies are distilled from the fermented mash of fruits, are generally white, and are not aged. Kirsch, framboise, Calvados or applejack, and mirabelle fall into this general category. Liqueurs are made by combining a spirit (often brandy) with one or a variety of flavorings and with sugar. For your home bar select three or four liqueurs from the following list: Amaretto, anisette, B&B, Benedictine, Chartreuse, Cointreau, crème de cacao, crème de cassis, crème de menthe (green; white is optional), curaçao, Drambuie, Galliano, Grand Marnier, Kahlúa, Midori, Tia Maria, or Triple Sec.

Liqueurs and fruit brandies are versatile and worthwhile investments, as both types of spirits can be used not only as after-dinner drinks but also in the creation of many coolers, mixed drinks, and desserts.

BUYING STRATEGIES

When purchasing liquor, there are several buying strategies worth considering. Well-known brands of spirits, particularly Scotch, bourbon, vodka, and gin, can be expensive. If you or your guests prefer drinking these potables neat or on the rocks, invest in good bottles. Consider buying house brands, however, for large parties or if you serve mixed drinks often. Many house brands are bottled by name-brand distilleries, and the products are remarkably similar in taste. Not every house brand is a bargain, but many are.

If you favor a particular brand of spirits, or know your guests do, think about buying it in larger bottles, such as a liter (a little more than a quart) or the 1.75 liter size (nearly a half gallon).

When you purchase liquor or wine by the case, you can almost always expect a discount. Discount rules for distilled spirits vary from state to state, but in most states a case of wine will be discounted at least 10 percent. Be sure to ask your vintner if a discount can be applied to your liquor or wine purchase.

Read and study the catalogues sent by liquor dealers. And do not overlook sales.

You may also want to stock some of the prepackaged drink mixes now available. To some you will have to add your own liquor. Many of these mixes are of excellent quality, but just as many are not. Experiment until you find a mix you like, although you will probably find it is more satisfying to make a drink from scratch.

MIXERS AND WATERS

The artfully mixed drink often depends on liquids that contain no alcohol. The most common mixers are club soda, tonic water, ginger ale, colas and diet sodas, and orange, tomato, and grapefruit juice. Use freshly squeezed fruit juices whenever possible.

Within the last few years imported and domestic mineral waters have gained in popularity not only as mixers but as beverages to be enjoyed on their own. Served straight up or on the rocks with a lemon twist, a slice of lime, or a strawberry, these waters are now preferred by many Americans to the once-favored soft drink and diet soda.

Bottled mineral waters fall into two categories: carbonated ("sparkling") and still. Well-known brands of sparkling waters include Apollinaris, Perrier, and San Pellegrino. Leaders in the still brands are Evian, Vittel, Fiuggi, and Deer Park. All should be served well chilled. A few have a distinct mineral flavor, others taste slightly alkaline, and some taste quite innocent.

So important have these waters become to the quenching of the national thirst that "water tastings" have been held in different parts of the country. In some of these blind trials on both coasts, Canada Dry club soda has won greater approval as a thirst quencher than many of the voguish, high-priced imports.

GARNISHES AND FLAVORINGS

Garnishes and flavorings are often added to mixed drinks. Some garnishes are vital—the onion in a Gibson or the lemon twist or olive in a Martini. Others, like the decorations on a cake, should be chosen for taste as well as their appeal to the eye. Freshly cut slices of lemon, lime, or orange are a fragrant and colorful addition to a tall summer cooler. Add raspberries and blueberries to a white-wine spritzer to salute the Fourth of July in style. Then, too, a thin slice of banana atop a banana Daiquiri or strawberry in a strawberry Daiquiri adds a special dimension to the drink. Transform a fine bottle of Finnish or Russian sipping vodka into a glacial delight by freezing it in a half-gallon milk carton. Place the bottle of vodka in the empty container, add water, and deep-freeze it. When the water has frozen, peel off the carton, wrap a handsome linen towel around the ice block, and pour from the icy bottle into shot glasses. It is high drama at its best.

Some flavorings are essential to balance the taste of a perfectly mixed drink. Grenadine, the bright red syrup made from pomegranates, is required in many cocktails, punches, and tall drinks. Bitters (Angostura or Peychaud's) are added to many mixed drinks to make them taste less sweet. And a Ramos Gin Fizz wouldn't be the same without its hint of orange flower water.

TOOLS OF
THE TRADE

Good bar equipment does not guarantee you will become an expert mixologist overnight, but it certainly helps you perform your tasks more efficiently. The most important tools you need are few in number and reasonably priced.

Check any bar equipment you may already have against this list of necessities:

- double-ended measure (one end to pour a jigger, 1½ ounces; the other a pony, 1 ounce)
- cocktail shaker with a sturdy mixing glass and metal shaker
- wire strainer
- set of measuring spoons
- long spoon or glass stirring rod (for mixing and stirring)
- corkscrew (sommelier's, lever action, or wing type)
- heavy-duty bottle and beer-can opener
- five-inch paring knife (for cutting and paring fresh fruit)
- bar muddler (for crushing sugar cubes or mint)
- heavy-duty lime squeezer
- lemon stripper
- small wooden cutting board
- two large pitchers with good pouring lips
- vacuum-type ice bucket and pair of ice tongs
- cocktail napkins and coasters, fabric or paper
- straws and toothpicks

Buy bar implements of good, professional quality. Begin collecting decanters, handsome additions to any bar. And consider using cloth cocktail napkins—they are colorful and available in easy-to-care-for fabrics. You might even want to splurge on an elegant silver jigger.

For mixing extra-special drinks, useful—though not essential—appliances are an electric blender or a food processor, an electric fruit juicer, and an ice crusher.

Opposite: Some basic bar equipment: pitcher with a good pouring lip and a glass stirring rod, wire strainer and mixing glass, lime squeezer, lemon stripper, small wooden cutting board, double-ended measure, bottle and beer-can opener, stirring spoon, coasters.

Joseph E. Seagram & Sons, Inc.

GLASSWARE

Photograph by Don Kushnick

Top row:
Cocktail glass (4 oz.),
cocktail glass (4 oz.),
sour glass (6 oz.),
collins glass (14 oz.),
highball glass (12 oz.),
old-fashioned glass (9 oz.).

Middle row:
Saucer champagne glass (6 oz.),
white wine glass (7 oz.),
balloon red wine glass (9 oz.),
Rhine wine or
Moselle wine glass (6 oz.),
tulip champagne glass (9 oz.).

Bottom row:
Liqueur glass (1 oz.),
liqueur glass (2 oz.),
liqueur glass (1 oz.),
pousse-café glass (1 oz.),
Irish coffee glass (6 oz.),
brandy snifter (10 oz.).

Today's styles and sizes of glasses vary widely, but basically they are either tumblers or stemware. Regardless of the quality of the glasses you select, be sure they are large enough for the kinds of drinks you intend to serve.

Start your glassware collection with at least a dozen of each of the following basic shapes: old-fashioned or on-the-rocks glasses (9-ounce), highball glasses (12-ounce), and all-purpose wine-glasses (10-ounce). Round out your collection with brandy snifters, tulip champagne glasses, or pilsner glasses. Let your style of entertaining be your guide. Use matching glassware at the dinner table, but for drinks before and after dinner an assortment of patterns is interesting. At an outdoor party plastic glasses are certainly appropriate. There are handsome, insulated ones available that will keep the ice significantly longer on hot days.

Top left:
Water goblet (10 oz.),
red wine glass (6 oz.),
white wine glass (7 oz.).

Top right:
Beer glass (12 oz.),
distinctive champagne glass
(6 oz.).

Bottom left:
A contemporary shot glass (1 oz.).

Bottom right:
Brandy snifters (8 oz., 2 oz.).

TECHNIQUES

Here are a few simple suggestions to make you a more proficient mixologist.

Always measure ingredients precisely. Never guess and never overpour; any change in proportions alters the taste of a drink.

Read the recipe carefully, and put the ingredients into the mixing glass or shaker in the order in which they are presented. Stir, shake, or strain drinks when called for. Stirring chills and mixes drinks; shaking blends them. When a carbonated mixer is added to a tall drink or cooler, stir it as briefly as possible to preserve its effervescence and sparkle.

Always serve drinks icy cold; in fact, the colder the better. If time permits, prechill your glasses, mixers, and spirits. It makes an enormous difference in your finished product. The simplest and easiest way to chill glasses is to place them in the refrigerator or freezer until cold. Use fresh ice and a clean glass for each round of drinks.

Put the ice in the glass or shaker before adding the ingredients; the liquids are then chilled as they are poured over ice.

Garnishing a drink is an art in itself. Garnishes are used for one of two reasons: Some, such as the twist of lemon in a dry Rob Roy, actually enhance the taste and flavor of the drink, others are simply ornaments added for color and/or flair.

Photograph by Sally Andersen-Bruce

Henry Zbrkiewicz, one of the expert mixologists at The "21" Club in New York City, concocts a Whiskey Sour.

Garnishes: celery rib, cucumber peel, whole cloves, horse's neck, half-slice of fresh lemon, orange-peel rose, scallion brush, fresh mint sprigs, cinnamon stick, cherry tomato, fresh strawberries with stems, maraschino cherry with stem, cocktail onion and olives, slices of fresh lime.

Photograph by Don Kushnick

Lemon, lime, and orange peels should be cut with a lemon stripper or a sharp paring knife just before they are used. If the peels sit around too long, the volatile oils dry up. The correct way to add a twist of citrus peel is to twist the peel over the drink first to release a drop of oil into it, then rub the rim of the glass with the peel, and, finally, drop it in the drink.

Another skill worth acquiring calls for a mixture of technique and showmanship: floating brandy, liqueurs, or cream. Floats depend on the density and gravity of liquids to be successful. To float brandy, liqueurs, cream, or other spirits, hold the bowl of a teaspoon a hair above the prepared drink or liqueur and pour the "float" slowly over the back of a spoon. You want the float to glide onto the top of the drink and settle there — much as oil floats on water.

Making a pousse-café, which involves the technique of floating liqueurs, is an art. Practice, and a little knowledge of the specific gravities of the required liqueurs, will ensure success. Follow pousse-café recipes to the letter, and float ingredients in the order in which they are given in the recipe.

19

An attractive (and necessary) garnish for a drink such as a Sidecar or Margarita is a glass frosted with sugar or salt. Frosting also adds a special touch when presenting coolers and liqueurs. Always use superfine sugar when frosting glasses. The technique is the same for both salt and sugar. Moisten the outer rim of the glass to about a depth of one-quarter inch with a wedge of lemon, lime, or orange, then dip the moistened rim in a saucer full of sugar or salt. Shake off any excess. For a colorful effect try moistening the rim of a glass to be sugar-frosted with grenadine. Glasses frosted with sugar or salt can be prepared ahead of time and kept in the refrigerator until needed.

The quality of a mixed drink depends not only on the happy marriage of its ingredients but also on accurate measuring. The following measurements are used in *The Art of Mixing Drinks:*

1 dash	3 drops
1 teaspoon	1/6 ounce
1 tablespoon (3 teaspoons)	½ ounce
1 pony	1 ounce
1 jigger	1½ ounces
1 cup	8 ounces
1 pint (½ quart)	16 ounces
1 fifth (4/5 quart)	25.6 ounces
1 quart	32 ounces
half gallon	64 ounces

When you use a recipe in this book (or any other book) for the first time, follow its instructions carefully. After you have mastered the recipe, you can decide how to change it to best suit your tastes. Perhaps you want to use more ice or a little less mixer. Or you might want to add an extra dash of Tabasco or bitters. There is only one rule about changing a drink recipe: Never change the drink's alcohol content. No one really appreciates a drink that is too strong, especially after the fact.

PARTY PRINCIPLES

The size and styles of parties change, but some fundamentals for giving them never do. They are: have plenty of ice on hand; place ashtrays where they can be seen and empty them often; and offer your guests a cup of coffee before they leave for home. The most important principle, however, is not to run out of liquor. It is always sound to have too much rather than too little; unopened bottles always keep, and many liquor stores will allow you to return them if you are a regular customer.

Buying liquor for an occasion such as a cocktail party, a sit-down dinner, or a big bash is different from buying wine and spirits for a home's basic bar. Before a party, decide on the drinks you will serve and, based on the number of guests you expect (and their drinking habits), determine the quantity of liquor you will need.

You can safely assume that each of your guests will have at least two or three cocktails, which means you will need two fifths for six to eight guests, three fifths for ten to twelve, five fifths for twenty, and eight fifths for thirty. If you purchase spirits by the quart (or liter) in the same quantities, there is a wider margin of safety.

When serving brandy and liqueurs, remember that most people have only one or two after-dinner drinks. Based on a one-ounce serving, plan on a fifth for twelve guests, two fifths for twenty, and three for thirty.

When wine is served with dinner, one person will usually drink two glasses with the meal. One bottle of wine serves three people, two bottles serve six, and four serve twelve. Four guests can be counted on to consume about two bottles of wine.

For further information, see the chart on page 92.

For mixing cocktails in quantity, simply multiply the ingredients by the number of requests for the drink. A good rule to follow is to put the number of glasses required in front of you before you begin to pour. This will help you keep track of the number of jiggers of gin, vodka, rum, or tequila you'll have to pour into the shaker or mixing glass.

COCKTAIL PARTY

A cocktail party can be anything from a small and informal get-together with a few close friends to an open-house celebration for more than a hundred at holiday time. Whether large or small, a cocktail party is fueled primarily by liquids and conversation.

The rules for giving a cocktail party are simple: Plan in advance, pay attention to details, extend a time-limited invitation, offer lots to drink and eat, and provide a setting that encourages your guests to enjoy themselves.

If you invite more than twenty people, send a written invitation at least two weeks in advance. Request that guests reply with "Regrets only." A cocktail party should last no longer than three hours, so be sure to specify the starting and ending time of your party in the invitation.

Prepare shopping lists and a shopping schedule. Pick up liquor, mixers, and all but fresh foodstuffs two days before the party.

Decide in advance on the best location for your bar. The number of guests you have invited, as well as the size of your home, will help you determine where to place it. If you expect a large group, set up bars on two different sides of the room — or, better yet, in two different rooms — to encourage circulation. Do not serve food from the bar. A bar for a crowd should be set up at a large, rectangular table, away from the wall so you or your bartender can stand behind it. Cover the table with a plastic dropcloth, and place a floor-length tablecloth over it.

Arrange wine and spirits on either side of the table, with ice, glasses, bar equipment, and mixers within easy reach. Keep reserves under the table, hidden from view. Ice can be stored in Styrofoam chests or in large watertight wastebaskets.

Essentials for a cocktail party are Scotch, rye or blended whiskey, vodka, gin, bourbon, beer, white wine, dry and sweet vermouth, mixers, and appropriate garnishes. Have fruit juices, bottled mineral waters, soft drinks (including diet ones), and soda available for nondrinkers. If you choose, have the fixings

Opposite: Casual set-up for a small and informal cocktail party.

for a limited number of fancy drinks, but remember you are giving a cocktail party and your guests will not expect you to serve exotic concoctions.

For a change of pace you may want to plan a cocktail party around a special drink or an occasion like Kentucky Derby Day — better yet, combine the two. Traditionally, Mint Juleps are served in silver tumblers. But if you do not own or cannot rent them, serve your Mint Juleps in silver-colored plastic tumblers. Or plan the festivities around a liquor-based punch like a Wassail Bowl, a snowy Eggnog, or a Fish House punch. During the summer, serve pitchers of Sangría, a rum-based cocktail, or Kir. Many of these libations can be prepared in advance and will lend themselves to self-service.

You will need at least twice as many glasses as you have guests. You may want to rent glasses if you are expecting a great many people. Avoid paper and Styrofoam cups — they are hard to handle and can alter the taste of a drink.

No one expects you to have a complete range of glasses for a cocktail party. The basic sizes should be fine. There are numerous styles of inexpensive, attractively designed glasses and plastic barware available today; if you give cocktail parties frequently, buy them by the case. An all-purpose wineglass is suitable for serving most drinks. At large affairs stemware is a good choice because you will find that coasters are not as necessary. It is always better to serve a drink in a glass that is too large rather than in one that is too small.

The food at a cocktail party can be as unpretentious or elaborate as your budget and ambitions dictate, but bite-sized portions and finger foods are essential. Crudités served with a curry or Roquefort-cheese dip, a selection of pâtés, sausages, and cheeses with an assortment of French breads, are simple, and delicious. Place the food in several locations or confine it to a separate table away from the bar. Wherever the food is served, put napkins beside it.

SIT-DOWN DINNER

The "pleasure of your company" is nowhere better expressed than at an intimate sit-down dinner. Invite guests by telephone two weeks in advance and, when extending the invitation, be specific about time — "sixish" is fine for a cocktail party, but not for dinner. Plan to begin serving the meal an hour and a half after the first guest arrives.

Selecting and presenting wines correctly can easily intimidate even the most accomplished host or hostess. If you are unsure about which wine to pour, discuss the menu with your vintner. It is his business to know and to recommend appropriate wines. The type of dish you are serving, as well as the manner in which you prepare it, should also be considered before making your selection. White wine with fish and poultry, red wine with red meats and game, is still a good rule to follow. Beer is more appropriate when served with spicy foods like chili con carne or curries, but a Gewürztraminer or a dry white Hermitage will hold its own against the hottest curry dish. At dinner, sherry appears only with the soup course. If fish or seafood is your starter, pour a crisp, dry white. A robust pâté de campagne would be delightful accompanied by a light-bodied red wine. Sweet white wines, such as a Sauterne or a Barsac, are delicious accompaniments to desserts. A semi-sweet champagne or a Vouvray is the perfect complement to a fruit course. (A dry or brut champagne should not be served at the close of a meal.)

If you plan to offer more than one wine at dinner, always pour white before red, dry before sweet, young before old, or light before full-bodied. The character, body, and bouquet of your wines will not be jeopardized, and the flavor of the food will be enhanced.

If you are planning on serving a white wine and a red wine with your meal, it will help to remember that the position of wine glasses at each place setting has been established by convention; any variation in this pattern may result in confusion for your guests. At a sit-down dinner, the water goblet is placed above the dinner knife, the glass for white wine to its right, and the glass for red wine behind the white wine glass.

Although wine glasses may remain at the table throughout the meal, it is a much better practice to remove each glass at the end of the course when possible.

Knowing how, when, and how much wine to pour can cause confusion, too. With a young wine like a Beaujolais, simply open the bottle, bring it to the table, and pour. White wines should be handled in the same way, but serve them chilled. Fine red wines require a little more attention to be at their best. Stand a bottle of good red wine right side up for a few hours if it has been in a wine rack, to allow any sediment to settle. An hour or two before serving, open the bottle and let the wine "breathe."

After removing the metal foil from the top of the bottle, wipe the cork and neck with a linen dish towel. Then uncork the bottle and wipe the inside of the bottle neck with a clean cloth before pouring. Fill glasses half full or even less, depending on the size — four ounces is a proper serving. When pouring, turn the bottle slightly to avoid drips.

After-dinner brandy and liqueurs can be served at the dining table or in the living room. If your guests are comfortable, and particularly if conversation is flowing well, do not break up the party. If conversation is lagging, however, a move to the living room is an opportunity to rearrange your guests and get things going again.

Opposite: Sumptuous and inviting, this table set for an intimate and elegant sit-down dinner expresses the good taste and gracious hospitality of the hostess.

Ruder & Finn/Lenox China, "Castle Garden"; Lenox Crystal, "Allure."

THE BIG BASH

The big bash is your opportunity to add a "second act" to your cocktail party in the form of a buffet brunch, lunch, or dinner.

A large party is usually time consuming and can be costly. Two things are key: planning, and putting your own personality into the event. Try a New Year's Day brunch, a Mardi Gras disco party, a Fourth of July antipasto picnic, a shared birthday celebration, or a Super Bowl supper—and turn it into *your* annual event. This is the way warm new traditions among good friends are born.

Planning for your bash should begin at least one month ahead of time (allow two months if your party will be held between Thanksgiving and New Year's Day). Your schedule should include: making arrangements for a caterer (if required), bartenders, and helpers; making up a guest list; selecting a theme (if you plan on using one); choosing decorations; constructing a menu; preparing shopping lists. Determine your budget, add approximately 25 percent for any unanticipated expenses, and start implementing your party plan.

The big bash, by definition, involves a large guest list—usually from twenty to forty people. Send written invitations three weeks in advance, and promise your guests cocktails and a meal. Specify "RSVP" or "Regrets only," and next to your telephone number—especially if you work—the best time to call.

A realistic timetable will make your big bash progress smoothly and efficiently. After you have sent out invitations and constructed your menu, it is time to take inventory. Figure out what kind of equipment you have and what you will have to rent or borrow. Your needs will be dictated by your menu, whether the party will be held indoors or out, and the season of the year. Enough plates for the main course and dessert, silver, napkins, glasses, and serving or presentation trays are essential. The liquors you choose will help you decide not only how many

Opposite: This charming outdoor setting for a big bash features seating for small groups. The food is placed conveniently so that guests may help themselves.

The Boulders Inn, New Preston, Connecticut. Photograph by Sally Andersen-Bruce

glasses you require but also the appropriate size and shape. You may want to rent tables and chairs, so all your guests can be seated in small groups of four or six. Have these items delivered the day before the party, to give you time to set them up. Only the purchase or delivery of fresh fish and flowers should be left for the party day.

If you know you will not be able to seat all your guests comfortably at one time, prepare a buffet menu that can be eaten easily without a knife. An elegant hot dish such as paella, stroganoff served with rice, or a well-flavored daube is a perfect lap food. Cold pasta salads made with tortellini or penne are also a welcome change. A macédoine of fresh fruits in season, an airy mousse made with white chocolate, and bite-sized pastries are toothsome desserts for a crowd.

Think of and orchestrate your large party as you would any three-course meal. For a luncheon or dinner you might want a full cocktail-party bar, followed by wine and bottled water offered with the meal and, possibly, brandy or liqueurs after dessert and coffee. For a brunch you will probably want to limit the drinks to Bloody Marys, Mimosas, Screwdrivers, or Tequila Sunrises.

You may enjoy your party more if you hire bartenders and helpers. A local junior college or university is a good place to look for help or you can turn to a local agency for temporary help.

Do not assume that the help you hire will know what you want them to do, when you would like it done, or where everything in your kitchen is located. Be sure your help arrives well before party time, and run them through the time and serving sequences you have established for your party. Alert them to all pouring, cleaning, and clearing duties you want them to perform. If you do that, you will be ready to greet your guests when the doorbell rings. Allow one hour for cocktails before you announce that "dinner is served." Now you can enjoy the atmosphere you have so carefully created.

Opposite: A group portrait of today's most popular mixed drinks.

Joseph E. Seagram & Sons, Inc.

COOLERS
AND
WATERS

Canada Dry

Cool and refreshing, these sparkling waters are colorfully garnished with fresh fruits of the season.

Americans, more calorie- and health-conscious than ever before, are now turning to new methods of quenching their thirst by concocting drinks based on sparkling mineral waters, tonic, and ginger ale. Cool, refreshing, light, and sparkling, these drinks can be served at any hour of the day or night — and in any climate. Particularly gratifying after a game of tennis or a three-mile run, an icy cooler will take the edge off any thirst. To get the most from your cooler, use a tall glass or a large wine goblet (the more it holds, the longer it will stay cold) and plenty of ice.

AMER PICON COOLER

1½ ounces Amer Picon
1 ounce gin
½ ounce cherry liqueur
½ ounce fresh lemon juice
1 teaspoon superfine sugar
club soda or sparkling mineral water

Shake well all ingredients, except
mixer, with ice. Strain into a tall glass
half filled with ice. Add club soda or
sparkling mineral water and stir
gently.

APPLE RUM COOLER

¾ ounce applejack or Calvados
¾ ounce light rum
1 wedge of lime
club soda
orange peel

Pour ingredients, except mixer, over
ice in a tall glass. Squeeze lime wedge
over drink and drop it into glass. Add
club soda and stir gently. Twist
orange peel over drink and drop into
the glass.

APRICOT COOLER

2 ounces apricot brandy
2 dashes grenadine
ginger ale or sparkling mineral water
one orange peel and one lemon peel

Pour ingredients, except mixer, into a
tall glass half filled with crushed ice
and stir. Add ginger ale or sparkling
mineral water and garnish with peels.

BLUE CLOUD

2 ounces Sambuca
1 ounce blue curaçao
club soda
1 slice each of orange and lemon
maraschino cherry

Pour ingredients, except mixer, over
crushed ice in a tall glass. Add club
soda and stir gently. Garnish with the
fruit slices and cherry.

BOCCIE BALL

1½ ounces Amaretto
1½ ounces fresh orange juice
2 ounces sparkling mineral water

Pour ingredients into a highball glass
filled with ice and stir gently.

BRIGHTON PUNCH

1 ounce bourbon
1 ounce brandy
¾ ounce Benedictine
1 ounce freshly squeezed orange
  juice
club soda
1 slice each of lemon and orange

Shake well all ingredients, except
mixer, with ice. Strain into an ice-filled
collins glass and add club soda. Stir
gently and garnish with the fruit slices.

BYRRH CASSIS COOLER

2 ounces Byrrh
½ ounce crème de cassis
sparkling mineral water
1 slice of lemon

Pour ingredients into an ice-filled tall
glass. Stir gently. Garnish with lemon.

CHAMPAGNE COOLER

1 ounce brandy
1 ounce Cointreau
6 ounces chilled brut champagne
fresh mint

Pour ingredients into a highball glass
half filled with crushed ice and stir
gently. Garnish with mint sprigs.

CHARTREUSE COOLER

1 ounce yellow Chartreuse
3 ounces fresh orange juice
1 ounce fresh lemon juice
bitter lemon
1 slice of orange

Shake well all ingredients, except
bitter lemon, with ice. Strain into a
tall glass half filled with ice, add bitter
lemon, and stir gently. Garnish with
the orange slice.

CLARET COOLER

4 ounces dry red wine
½ ounce brandy
1 ounce fresh orange juice
½ ounce fresh lemon juice
3 ounces sparkling mineral water
1 slice of lemon
1 orange peel

Pour ingredients into a tall glass filled
with crushed ice and stir gently. Garnish with lemon slice and orange peel.

COFFEE COOLER

4 ounces strong, cold coffee
1½ ounces vodka
1 ounce coffee liqueur
1 teaspoon superfine sugar
1 scoop coffee ice cream

Shake well all ingredients, except ice cream, with ice. Strain into a tall glass and add ice cream.

COUNTRY CLUB COOLER

3 ounces dry vermouth
1 teaspoon grenadine
sparkling mineral water or club soda

Pour ingredients into a tall glass filled with ice and stir gently.

CRANBERRY COOLER

2 ounces cranberry liqueur
sparkling mineral water or club soda
1 slice of orange

Pour liqueur over ice in a tall glass, add mixer and stir gently. Garnish with the orange slice.

CURAÇAO COOLER

1 ounce blue curaçao
1 ounce vodka
½ ounce fresh lime juice
½ ounce fresh lemon juice
fresh orange juice
1 peel each of lemon, lime, and
　orange

Shake well all ingredients, except orange juice, with ice. Strain into a tall glass half filled with ice cubes, add orange juice, and stir. Twist each peel above drink and drop into glass.

DRY MANHATTAN COOLER

2 ounces blended whiskey
1 ounce dry vermouth
2 ounces fresh orange juice
½ ounce fresh lemon juice
½ ounce orgeat
club soda or sparkling mineral water
1 maraschino cherry

Shake well all ingredients, except mixer, with ice. Strain into a tall glass half filled with ice, add a splash of sparkling mineral water, and stir gently. Garnish with the maraschino cherry.

DUBONNET COOLER

1½ ounces Dubonnet
1½ ounces Dubonnet blonde
sparkling mineral water
½ fresh lime
fresh mint

Pour ingredients into a tall glass half filled with ice and stir gently. Squeeze lime into drink and add the shell. Garnish with mint sprigs.

FLORADORA

2 ounces gin
3 tablespoons fresh lime juice
½ teaspoon superfine sugar
1 tablespoon raspberry syrup
2 ounces sparkling mineral water or
　ginger ale

Pour ingredients into a tall glass half filled with crushed ice and stir gently.

HARVARD COOLER

2 ounces Calvados or applejack
½ teaspoon superfine sugar
club soda or ginger ale
1 orange peel

Pour ingredients, except mixer, into a tall glass and stir to dissolve sugar. Add ice cubes and club soda or ginger ale and garnish with orange peel.

HIGHLAND COOLER

2½ ounces Scotch
2 dashes Angostura bitters
2 tablespoons fresh lemon juice
1 teaspoon superfine sugar
ginger ale

Pour ingredients, except mixer, into a tall glass filled with ice cubes and stir. Add ginger ale.

IRISH COOLER

3 ounces Irish whiskey
1 lemon peel
club soda or sparkling mineral water

Pour ingredients, except mixer, into a tall glass filled with ice cubes. Add club soda or sparkling mineral water and stir gently. Garnish with lemon peel.

MANHATTAN COOLER

4 ounces dry red wine
3 dashes rum
2 tablespoons fresh lemon juice
1½ teaspoons superfine sugar
1 slice each of lemon and orange

Pour all ingredients into an ice-filled glass and stir. Garnish with lemon and orange slices.

NEGRONI COOLER

1½ ounces sweet vermouth
1½ ounces Campari
1½ ounces gin
sparkling mineral water
1 slice of orange

Pour ingredients, except mixer, into a tall glass filled with ice cubes. Add sparkling mineral water and stir gently. Garnish with orange slice.

PINEAPPLE MINT COOLER

2 ounces gin
½ ounce white crème de menthe
3 ounces pineapple juice
1 ounce fresh lemon juice
sparkling mineral water
fresh pineapple stick and green
  cherry

Shake all ingredients, except mixer, and strain into a tall, ice-filled glass. Add sparkling mineral water and stir gently. Garnish with fresh pineapple and cherrry.

REMSEN COOLER

½ teaspoon superfine sugar
2 ounces club soda
2 ounces gin
ginger ale
1 lemon peel

Dissolve sugar with the club soda in a tall glass, add ice cubes and gin, and stir. Fill with ginger ale and garnish the drink with lemon peel.

ROCK AND RYE COOLER

1½ ounces vodka
1 ounce rock and rye
½ ounce fresh lime juice
bitter lemon
1 slice of lime

Shake well all ingredients, except mixer, with ice. Strain into an ice-filled collins glass and add bitter lemon. Stir gently and garnish with the slice of lime.

ROMAN COOLER

1½ ounces gin
½ ounce Punt e Mes
½ ounce fresh lemon juice
1 teaspoon superfine sugar
sparkling mineral water
1 lemon peel

Shake well all ingredients, except mixer, with ice. Strain into a tall, ice-filled glass and add sparkling mineral water. Twist peel above the drink and drop it into the glass.

VERMOUTH COOLER

2 ounces dry vermouth
2 tablespoons raspberry syrup
sparkling mineral water
1 slice of orange

Pour ingredients into a tall glass filled with ice cubes and stir gently to mix. Garnish with orange slices.

WHITE CLOUD

1 ounce Sambuca
club soda or sparkling mineral water
1 slice of lime

Pour Sambuca over ice in a tall glass, add mixer and stir gently. Garnish with the slice of lime.

WHITE WINE SPRITZER

4 ounces dry white wine
sparkling mineral water
1 lemon peel

Pour wine into a tall glass or large goblet, add ice cubes and sparkling mineral water, and stir gently. Twist lemon peel above drink and drop it into the glass.

  Other attractive and colorful garnishes for this drink include fresh fruits in season such as strawberries, raspberries, melon balls, peeled seedless grapes, and blueberries.

WINE COOLER

2 teaspoons superfine sugar
1 teaspoon water
1 tablespoon fresh orange juice
red or white wine
1 slice of lemon or orange

Pour ingredients into a tall glass and stir to dissolve sugar. Fill glass with ice cubes and garnish a red-wine cooler with lemon slice, a white-wine cooler with orange slice.

NONALCOHOLIC BEVERAGES

Beautiful eggnogs blended of fresh fruits, milk, eggs, honey, and club soda.

The universal popularity of soft drinks tells a simple story. There are a lot of people thirsty for beverages containing no alcohol. Be prepared to serve a nonalcoholic drink to any guest who may request one, and remember that it need not be boring. Present the drink in an attractive glass and take the time to garnish it nicely. Requests may range from a Pussyfoot (known as a Shirley Temple in some circles), to a Virgin Mary, to a plain glass of tonic over ice with a lime wedge. Simple though the drink may be, if you treat it with as much style and flair as you do any cocktail, your guests will feel well taken care of.

ANGOSTURA HIGHBALL

1 teaspoon Angostura bitters
ginger ale
maraschino cherry
1 slice of orange

Pour ingredients into an ice-filled highball glass and stir gently. Garnish with the cherry and orange slice.

BANANA EGGNOG

3 cups whole milk, chilled
1 cup mashed bananas
2 eggs
4 ice cubes
1 tablespoon honey
1 cup club soda

Mix milk, bananas, ice cubes, and honey in an electric blender or food processor. Whirl at medium speed for about 30 seconds. Pour in club soda just before serving and stir to blend. Garnish with banana slices. To make a lime or tomato eggnog, substitute ½ cup lime or tomato juice for the mashed bananas, and garnish with a lime wheel or cherry tomato. Serves 4.

BOSTON TOMATO JUICE COCKTAIL

1 cup tomato or V-8 juice
½ cup clam juice
1½ tablespoons fresh lime juice
dash of Tabasco sauce
salt to taste

Pour ingredients into a blender and blend for one minute. Serve in a tall, ice-filled glass.

GRAPE FOLLY

white or red grape juice
sparkling mineral water
¼ lime

Put ice cubes in a tall glass and fill one third full with white or red grape juice. Top with sparkling mineral water, squeeze lime into drink, add shell, and stir gently.

ORANGE SPARKLE

3 ounces freshly squeezed orange
    juice
seltzer or sparkling mineral water
1 slice of orange

Pour ingredients over ice into an old-fashioned glass and stir gently. Garnish with the slice of orange.

PERFECT CASSIS LEMONADE

4 tablespoons fresh lemon juice
1½ ounces sirop de cassis
1 cup sparkling mineral water or
    plain water

Pour ingredients into a tall, ice-filled glass and stir.

PUSSYFOOT

4 ounces ginger ale
½ teaspoon grenadine
1 lemon peel
1 slice of orange

Pour all ingredients into an ice-filled old-fashioned glass and stir gently. Garnish with lemon peel and orange slice.

REALLY ROSY

2 tablespoons fresh lemon juice
1 tablespoon grenadine
sparkling mineral water

Pour ingredients, except mixer, into a tall, ice-filled glass. Add sparkling mineral water and stir gently.

SARATOGA

2 tablespoons fresh lemon juice
½ teaspoon superfine sugar
2 dashes Angostura bitters
ginger ale

Put ingredients, except ginger ale, into a tall, ice-filled glass and stir to dissolve sugar. Add ginger ale.

SUMMER SIPPER

3 tablespoons fresh lime juice
¾ ounce raspberry syrup
sparkling mineral water
fresh raspberries and slice of lime

Pour ingredients into a tall, ice-filled glass and stir to mix. Garnish with fresh raspberries and lime slice.

TOMATO JUICE ITALIAN STYLE

1 cup tomato juice
4 leaves fresh basil
¼-inch slice of red onion
salt and pepper to taste

Pour ingredients into a blender and blend for one minute. Serve in a tall, ice-filled glass.

APERITIFS

A refreshing variation on a classic theme—the Dubonnet Manhattan. An equally exciting libation can be made with rum.

The classic aperitifs are dry sherry and sweet and dry vermouth. The others, bitter or sweet, are subtle (and often secret) blends of herbs and spices, roots and barks, quinine, wine, or brandy. Dubonnet (red or white) is one of the best known French aperitifs. Red is the sweeter of the two, and the addition of a slice of lemon will give it a touch of tartness. Other French favorites are Lillet (red or white), St.-Raphaël (red or white), and Byrrh (pronounced *beer*). The most famous Italian aperitif is Campari (a bitter) and it makes a lovely drink when combined with club soda over ice. Two other Italian aperitifs that contain quinine are Punt e Mes and Cynar (pronounced *she-nar*)—made from artichokes. Aperitifs based on aniseed are Pernod and Ricard from France and ouzo from Greece. Far from mild, these aperitifs are stronger than brandy, and must be diluted with water or club soda before serving. This addition will transform aniseed aperitifs from clear liquids to cloudy, milky ones.

ADONIS

2 ounces dry sherry
1 ounce sweet vermouth
dash of orange bitters

Pour all ingredients into a mixing glass filled with ice and stir. Strain into a cocktail glass.

AMBROSIA

1 lump sugar
3 dashes Angostura bitters
1 ounce cognac
4 ounces chilled brut champagne

Put sugar in a tulip champagne glass and moisten it with bitters. Pour in remaining ingredients, adding champagne slowly, waiting for foam to subside before continuing to pour.

AMERICANO

3 ounces sweet vermouth
1½ ounces Campari
1 orange peel

Pour all ingredients into a mixing glass filled with ice and stir. Strain into a cocktail glass and garnish with orange peel.

AMER PICON ON-THE-ROCKS

1½ ounces Amer Picon
½ ounce fresh lemon juice
sparkling mineral water
1 slice of lemon

Pour ingredients, except mixer, into an ice-filled old-fashioned glass. Add a splash of sparkling mineral water and stir gently. Garnish with lemon.

BITTERSWEET

1½ ounces sweet vermouth
1½ ounces dry vermouth
1 dash Angostura bitters
1 dash orange bitters
orange peel

Pour all ingredients into a mixing glass filled with cracked ice and stir well. Strain into a chilled cocktail glass. Twist orange peel over drink and drop it into the glass.

BONFIRE

1 ounce Punt e Mes
2 ounces cognac
1 ounce Calvados or applejack
lemon peel

Pour all ingredients into a mixing glass filled with ice and stir. Strain into a chilled cocktail glass. Twist lemon peel over drink and drop it into the glass.

BRAZIL

1½ ounces sherry
1½ ounces dry vermouth
1 dash Pernod
1 dash Angostura bitters
1 lemon twist

Pour all ingredients into a mixing glass filled with ice and stir. Strain into a cocktail glass and add lemon twist.

BROKEN SPUR

3 ounces white port
½ ounce gin
½ ounce sweet vermouth
1 egg yolk
1 teaspoon anisette

Shake all ingredients vigorously with ice. Strain into a large, chilled wine glass.

BYRRH CASSIS

1½ ounces Byrrh
¼ ounce crème de cassis
½ ounce fresh lemon juice
1 lemon slice

Shake all ingredients well with ice. Strain into an ice-filled old-fashioned glass and garnish with lemon slice.

BYRRH COCKTAIL

1½ ounces Byrrh
1½ ounces gin
1 lemon peel

Pour ingredients into a mixing glass filled with ice and stir. Strain into an ice-filled old-fashioned glass, twist peel over drink, and drop it into glass.

CAMPARI AND GIN

1¼ ounces Campari
1¼ ounces gin
1 orange peel

Pour ingredients into a mixing glass filled with ice and stir. Strain into an ice-filled old-fashioned glass, twist peel over drink, and drop it into glass.

CAMPARI AND LIME

1½ ounces Campari
quinine water
lime wedge
1 teaspoon freshly squeezed lime
    juice

Pour Campari over ice in a tall glass,
add the lime wedge and juice. Fill with
quinine water and stir gently.

CAMPARI AND SODA

1½ ounces Campari
club soda
lemon peel

Pour Campari over ice in a tall glass,
add club soda, and stir gently. Twist
peel over drink and drop into glass.

CAPRI COCKTAIL

2 ounces Campari
1 ounce vodka
2 drops Angostura bitters
1 teaspoon superfine sugar (or
    to taste)
lemon peel

Shake all ingredients well with
cracked ice and strain into a chilled
cocktail glass. Twist lemon peel over
drink and drop into glass.

CARDINAL

¾ ounce gin
¾ ounce Campari
¾ ounce dry vermouth
1 lemon peel

Pour ingredients into a mixing glass
filled with ice and stir. Strain into a
cocktail glass, twist peel over drink,
and drop it into glass.

CHAMPAGNE FRAISE

½ teaspoon strawberry liqueur
½ teaspoon kirsch
4 ounces chilled brut champagne
1 fresh strawberry with stem
    attached

Pour liqueur and kirsch into a chilled
tulip champagne glass and tilt to coat
the inside of the glass. Add champagne and garnish with strawberry.

CINZANO

3 ounces Cinzano sweet vermouth
2 dashes orange bitters
2 dashes Angostura bitters
1 orange peel

Pour all ingredients into a mixing
glass filled with ice and stir. Strain
into a cocktail glass, twist peel over
drink, and drop it into glass.

CLARET LEMONADE

4 tablespoons fresh lemon juice
2 teaspoons superfine sugar
8 ounces chilled claret or other dry
    red wine
1 slice of lemon

Put sugar and lemon juice in a tall
glass and stir to dissolve sugar. Add
claret, fill glass with crushed ice, and
garnish with the lemon slice.

CORONATION

¾ ounce dry vermouth
1 ounce Dubonnet
1 ounce gin

Pour all ingredients into a mixing
glass filled with ice and stir. Strain
into a cocktail glass.

CYNAR COCKTAIL

2 ounces Cynar
2 ounces sweet vermouth
1 slice of orange

Pour ingredients over ice into an old-
fashioned glass. Stir gently and garnish with the orange slice.

DEVIL

1½ ounces port
1½ ounces dry vermouth
2 dashes fresh lemon juice

Pour all ingredients into a mixing
glass filled with ice and stir. Strain
into a cocktail glass.

DIPLOMAT

3 ounces dry vermouth
1 ounce sweet vermouth
dash maraschino
maraschino cherry
1 lemon peel

Pour all ingredients into a mixing
glass filled with ice and stir well.
Strain into a cocktail glass, twist peel
over drink, and drop it into glass.
Garnish with the cherry.

DUBONNET
MANHATTAN

1½ ounces Dubonnet
1½ ounces blended whiskey
1 slice of lemon
maraschino cherry

Pour ingredients into a mixing glass
filled with ice and stir well. Strain into
a chilled cocktail glass and garnish
with the cherry and lemon slice.

EAST INDIA COCKTAIL

1½ ounces sweet sherry
1½ ounces dry vermouth
1 dash orange bitters

Shake ingredients well with ice and strain into a chilled sherry glass.

ITALIAN COCKTAIL

3 ounces Punt e Mes
dash dry vermouth
dash Campari
wedge of lemon
1 lemon slice

Pour ingredients into a large wineglass filled with ice and squeeze the lemon wedge over the drink. Garnish with the lemon slice.

KIR

4 ounces chilled dry white wine
½ ounce crème de cassis

Pour ingredients into a chilled wineglass. Add ice cubes if desired.

KIR ROYALE

4 ounces chilled brut champagne
½ ounce crème de cassis

Pour ingredients into a chilled tulip champagne glass.

LILLET COCKTAIL

2 ounces Lillet
1 ounce gin
1 lemon peel

Pour ingredients into a mixing glass filled with ice and stir. Strain into a cocktail glass. Twist peel over drink and drop it into glass.

MACARONI

1½ ounces Pernod
½ ounce sweet vermouth

Shake all ingredients vigorously with ice. Strain into a chilled cocktail glass.

MARY GARDEN

1½ ounces Dubonnet
1½ ounces dry vermouth

Pour ingredients into a mixing glass filled with ice and stir well. Strain into a cocktail glass.

MIMOSA

3 ounces freshly squeezed orange juice
3 ounces chilled brut champagne

Pour ingredients into a chilled tulip champagne glass.

MOONSHINE COCKTAIL

½ ounce Dubonnet blonde
½ ounce brandy
½ ounce peach-flavored brandy
1 dash Pernod

Shake all ingredients well with ice and strain into a chilled cocktail glass.

NEGRONI

1½ ounces sweet vermouth
1½ ounces Campari
1½ ounces gin
1 lemon peel

Pour ingredients into an old-fashioned glass filled with ice and stir. Twist peel over drink and drop it into glass.

PANSY

1½ ounces Pernod
6 dashes grenadine
2 dashes Angostura bitters

Shake all ingredients vigorously with ice. Strain into a chilled cocktail glass.

PEPI GENDI

1½ ounces tequila
2 dashes Benedictine
juice of one small lime
lime peel, cut in a long spiral

Shake all ingredients well with ice. Strain into a chilled cocktail glass and garnish with the lime spiral.

PICON

1½ ounces Amer Picon
1½ ounces dry vermouth
lemon peel

Pour ingredients into a mixing glass filled with ice and stir. Strain into a cocktail glass. Twist peel over drink and drop into glass.

PICON GRENADINE

1½ ounces Amer Picon
¾ ounce grenadine
chilled club soda
1 slice of orange

Pour ingredients into an old-fashioned glass half filled with ice, add club soda, and stir gently. Garnish with the orange slice.

PUNT E MES NEGRONI

1½ ounces Punt e Mes
1½ ounces sweet vermouth
1½ ounces gin
1 lemon peel

Pour ingredients into an old-fashioned glass filled with ice and stir. Twist peel over drink and drop it into glass.

QUEBEC

½ ounce dry vermouth
1½ teaspoons Amer Picon
1½ teaspoons maraschino
1½ ounces Canadian whisky

Shake all ingredients thoroughly with ice and strain into a cocktail glass rimmed with sugar.

ROLLS ROYCE

½ ounce dry vermouth
½ ounce sweet vermouth
1½ ounces gin
¼ teaspoon Benedictine

Pour ingredients into a mixing glass filled with ice and stir. Strain into a chilled cocktail glass.

ST.-RAPHAËL AND VODKA

3 ounces St.-Raphaël
1½ ounces vodka
sparkling mineral water
1 lemon peel

Pour ingredients, except mixer, into a large wineglass filled with ice. Add a splash of sparkling mineral water and stir gently. Twist peel over drink and drop it into glass.

SANCTUARY

2 ounces Dubonnet
1 ounce Amer Picon
1 ounce Cointreau

Shake all the ingredients well with ice. Strain into an old-fashioned glass filled with ice.

SAN GENNARO

1½ ounces Cynar
1½ ounces vodka
1 dash sweet vermouth
1 orange slice

Pour ingredients over ice into an old-fashioned glass. Stir well and garnish with the orange slice.

SHERRY COCKTAIL

2½ ounces sherry
1 dash Angostura bitters
orange peel

Shake ingredients thoroughly with ice and strain into a chilled cocktail glass. Twist peel over drink and drop into glass.

SHERRY TWIST

1 ounce sherry
½ ounce brandy
½ ounce dry vermouth
½ ounce Triple Sec
½ teaspoon fresh lemon juice
orange peel
cinnamon

Shake all ingredients thoroughly with ice and strain into a chilled cocktail glass. Twist peel over drink and drop into glass. Top with a pinch of cinnamon.

SLOE VERMOUTH

1 ounce sloe gin
1 ounce dry vermouth
1 ounce fresh lemon juice

Shake all ingredients well with ice and strain into a cocktail glass.

SMILER COCKTAIL

½ ounce sweet vermouth
½ ounce dry vermouth
1 ounce gin
1 dash Angostura bitters
¼ teaspoon fresh orange juice

Shake ingredients thoroughly with ice and strain into a chilled cocktail glass.

SOUL KISS COCKTAIL

1½ teaspoons Dubonnet
1½ teaspoons fresh orange juice
¾ ounce dry vermouth
¾ ounce bourbon

Shake ingredients well with ice and strain into a chilled cocktail glass.

STRAIGHT LAW COCKTAIL

1½ ounces dry sherry
¾ ounce gin

Pour ingredients into a mixing glass filled with ice and stir. Strain into a chilled cocktail glass.

SUISSESSE

1½ ounces Pernod
4 dashes anisette
1 egg white

Shake all ingredients thoroughly with ice and strain into a chilled cocktail glass.

VERMOUTH CASSIS

3 ounces dry vermouth
1 ounce crème de cassis
sparkling mineral water
1 slice of lemon

Pour all ingredients into a tall glass filled with ice and stir gently. Garnish with the lemon slice.

VERMOUTH COCKTAIL

1 ounce sweet vermouth
1 ounce dry vermouth
1 dash orange bitters
maraschino cherry

Pour ingredients into a mixing glass filled with ice and stir. Strain into a chilled cocktail glass and garnish with the cherry.

VERMOUTH HALF AND HALF

1½ ounces dry vermouth
1½ ounces sweet vermouth
chilled club soda
lemon peel

Pour vermouth into a mixing glass filled with ice and stir. Strain into a chilled wine goblet and add club soda. Twist lemon peel over drink and drop it into the glass.

One of the most pleasant and satisfying of aperitifs: a glass of fine Amontillado sherry.

VERMOUTH TRIPLE SEC

1 ounce dry vermouth
½ ounce Triple Sec
1 ounce gin
2 dashes orange bitters
1 lemon peel

Shake all ingredients well with ice and strain into a cocktail glass. Twist peel over drink and drop it into glass.

WHISPERS OF THE FROST

¾ ounce port
¾ ounce sherry
¾ ounce blended whiskey
1 slice each of lemon and orange

Pour ingredients into a mixing glass filled with ice and stir until well chilled. Strain into a cocktail glass and garnish with the fruit slices.

PUNCH

Photograph by Taylor Lewis

Snowy Eggnog, dusted with freshly grated nutmeg, festively served during the Christmas season in a handsome silver punchbowl.

The classic accompaniment to any large gathering for a special occasion is that versatile potable known as punch.

Punches have been popular with crowds for centuries; George Washington's favorite was Fish House punch. This potent libation originated at a fishing and social club in Pennsylvania in the mid-eighteenth century. Based on rum and peach-flavored brandy, it is a welcome and heady thirst quencher to be enjoyed in spring and summer.

In twelfth-century England, a response to the toast "wassail" was "drink hail." This toast was used during the holiday season, and by the sixteenth century it had given its name to the spicy brew that became the Wassail Bowl.

ARTILLERY PUNCH

1 quart bourbon
1¼ cups light rum
½ cup dark rum
⅔ cup apricot brandy
1½ cups freshly squeezed lemon juice
3 cups freshly squeezed orange juice
1 quart cold, strong black tea
¼ cup superfine sugar
lemon peels

Pour all ingredients into a punch bowl and stir to dissolve the sugar. Put a large block of ice in the bowl. Let flavors marry for an hour before serving. Garnish with lemon peels. Serves 30.

AZTEC PUNCH

2 quarts tequila
1½ cups freshly squeezed lemon juice
½ cup superfine sugar
2 26-ounce cans grapefruit juice
1 quart cold, strong black tea
¾ teaspoon ground cinnamon

Combine all ingredients and allow flavors to marry for an hour before serving. Pour over a large block of ice in a punch bowl. Serves 60.

BORDELAISE CHAMPAGNE PUNCH

3 bottles chilled brut champagne
1 bottle Lillet
orange peels

Pour champagne over ice in a large punch bowl and add Lillet to taste. Garnish with orange peels. Serves 18.

CASSIS PUNCH

2 cups fresh whole strawberries, hulled
½ cup crème de cassis
3 bottles dry white wine or brut champagne

Pour the cassis over the strawberries. Let stand for an hour to macerate strawberries. Strain the cassis over a large block of ice in a punch bowl. Reserve the strawberries. Add wine or champagne and stir gently. Garnish with strawberries. Serves 20.

CHAMPAGNE PUNCH

6 lumps sugar
dash of orange bitters
1 cup fine cognac
3 bottles chilled brut champagne

Put sugar lumps in a punch bowl and add a dash of bitters. Add cognac. Stir to dissolve the sugar. Just before serving, add a large block of ice and pour in champagne. Garnish with fresh fruits in season if desired. Serves 20.

CLARET PUNCH

1 cup superfine sugar
3 cups freshly squeezed lemon juice
1 cup white curaçao
2 cups brandy
3 bottles claret
1 quart sparkling mineral water

Dissolve sugar in lemon juice and pour over a large block of ice in a punch bowl. Add remaining ingredients and stir gently. Garnish with fresh fruits in season if desired. Serves 40.

CRANBERRY AND PLUM COOLER

1 fifth plum wine
1 fifth vodka
1 quart cranberry juice cocktail
1 quart club soda
1 quart 7-Up
1 tray ice cubes made by adding a drop of grenadine to each cube before freezing

Pour all ingredients into a large punch bowl. Add a block of ice and the grenadine-flavored ice cubes. Stir gently. Serves 36.

EGGNOG

12 eggs, separated
1½ cups superfine sugar
1 quart heavy cream
1 quart milk
1 quart bourbon or brandy
½ teaspoon salt
nutmeg

Beat the egg yolks and sugar until thick and lemon-colored. In a separate bowl, whip the cream until stiff, add milk, and slowly stir in the bourbon or brandy. Combine the mixtures in a large punch bowl. Beat the egg whites with the salt until stiff and fold gently into the eggnog. Dust with freshly grated nutmeg. Serves 30.

Prepared eggnog, available during the holiday season in most grocery stores can be a lifesaver when guests drop in unexpectedly. To enliven the mix, add the following ingredients per quart: 6 ounces bourbon, 3 ounces brandy, and 3 ounces light or dark rum. Dust each serving with freshly grated nutmeg.

FISH HOUSE PUNCH

1½ cups superfine sugar
4 cups cold water
1 fifth cognac or fine brandy
1 fifth golden rum
1 fifth dark rum
3 cups freshly squeezed lemon juice
⅔ cup peach brandy

Put sugar in a punch bowl with 2 cups of the water and stir until it is dissolved. Add remaining ingredients and allow flavors to marry for at least one hour, stirring occasionally. Just before serving, add a large block of ice to the punch bowl. Serves 40.

GLÖGG

3 whole cardamom seeds
8 whole cloves
2 tablespoons freshly grated orange
   peel
¾ cup water
¼ cup blanched almonds
½ cup raisins
1 bottle red wine
1 bottle port
1¾ cups vodka
superfine sugar to taste

Put the spices and orange peel in a cheesecloth bag and tie it. Bring the water to a boil and add almonds, raisins, and the spices. Simmer gently for 25 minutes. In a large stainless-steel pot bring the wine, port, and vodka to a boil with the fruits and spices. Remove the pot from the heat and allow it to cool. Store in the refrigerator for at least 12 hours. Just before serving, remove the spice bag, reheat mixture, and add superfine sugar to taste. Serves 20.

HARVARD MILK PUNCH

2 quarts whole milk
1 pint coffee ice cream
⅔ cup bourbon
⅓ cup rum

Blend ingredients in several batches in an electric blender until smooth. Pour into 6-ounce punch cups. Serves 14.

HOT-BLOODED MARY

1 quart tomato juice
½ cup freshly squeezed lemon juice
2 teaspoons horseradish, drained
3 dashes Worcestershire sauce
3 dashes Tabasco sauce
1½ cups vodka or gin
1 green pepper, seeded, cored, and
   cut into eight strips

Combine all ingredients, except vodka or gin and green pepper, in a large saucepan and simmer for five minutes. Pour 1½ ounces of gin or vodka into each of 8 heatproof mugs. Add some of the warmed tomato juice mixture to each mug, stir, and garnish with the green pepper strips. Serves 8.

HOT CHRISTMAS PUNCH

2 gallons fresh apple cider
2 cups light rum
2 lemons, peeled and sliced
2 oranges, peeled and sliced
10 cinnamon sticks
1 tablespoon ground cinnamon
1 tablespoon nutmeg
10 whole cloves

Put ingredients into a large pot or casserole and heat to the boiling point. Serves 20.

HOT RED-WINE PUNCH

2 fifths dry red wine
1 cup ruby port
⅓ cup brandy
3 3-inch sticks cinnamon
1 tablespoon whole cloves
½ teaspoon ground ginger
¼ teaspoon allspice
3 limes, thinly sliced
superfine sugar
1 dash Angostura bitters

Put all ingredients into a large saucepan or pot and add sugar to taste. Heat through, but do not boil. Ladle into 10 heatproof mugs. Serves 10.

MAY BOWL

1 quart fresh strawberries, hulled
7 tablespoons superfine sugar
3 bottles chilled Moselle wine
1 bottle chilled brut champagne

Sprinkle the strawberries with the sugar and pour 1 bottle of Moselle over them and refrigerate for 3 hours. Just before serving, put a large block of ice in a punch bowl and add the strawberry-wine mixture and the remaining ingredients. Stir gently. Serves 25.

MULLED WINE

1 quart burgundy
peel from 1 lemon and 1 orange
3-inch stick of cinnamon
1 whole nutmeg, crushed
6 whole cloves
1 tablespoon superfine sugar

Combine all ingredients in a stainless-steel pot and simmer gently for eight minutes. Strain and serve in warmed mugs. Serves 12.

ROYAL PURPLE PUNCH

2 bottles claret
2 quarts ginger ale
lemon slices studded with cloves

Pour ingredients over ice cubes in a large punch bowl and stir gently. Float the lemon slices on top. Serves 24.

RUM PARTY PUNCH

2 cups freshly squeezed orange juice
2 cups unsweetened pineapple juice
2 cups club soda
3 ounces freshly squeezed lime juice
2 cups light rum
superfine sugar

Pour all ingredients into a large punch bowl, add sugar to taste, and stir until sugar dissolves. Add a block of ice. Serves 12.

SANGRÍA

1 bottle Spanish red wine
1 orange, thinly sliced
6 lemon slices
1½ ounces cognac or brandy
1 ounce Triple Sec
1 ounce maraschino
1 tablespoon superfine sugar (or to taste)
6 ounces sparkling mineral water

Put all the ingredients, except mixer, into a large pitcher and stir to dissolve the sugar. Let flavors marry for at least an hour. Just before serving, add sparkling mineral water and ice cubes to the pitcher and stir gently. Pour into chilled wineglasses. Makes 8 6-ounce drinks.

SPARKLING MELON PUNCH

1 fifth Midori
1 fifth light rum
12 ounces crème de banane
1 46-ounce can unsweetened pineapple juice
12 ounces Rose's lime juice
1½ quarts chilled club soda
1 lime, thinly sliced (optional)
1 pint strawberries, sliced (optional)

Pour all ingredients into a large punch bowl and stir to combine. Add a large block of ice to the bowl. Garnish with the sliced fruit. Serves 40.

For a spectacular summertime presentation of this punch, make a watermelon punch bowl. Slice off the top third of a large watermelon, and scoop out the flesh. Save it for another use. Chill the "punch bowl" for several hours. Mix the punch, as directed, in a large bowl and ladle it into the cold melon shell over large chunks of ice.

SUMMER PUNCH COOLER

3 cups apricot nectar
2 pints orange sherbet
1 bottle chilled brut champagne
2 ounces Grand Marnier

Blend apricot nectar and orange sherbet in several batches in an electric blender until smooth. Let mixture stand in the refrigerator until ready to serve. Place a block of ice in a large punch bowl, and pour the mixture over it. Add the champagne and Grand Marnier and stir gently. Serves 12.

WASSAIL BOWL

12 small apples, cored
12 teaspoons dark brown sugar
1 cup superfine sugar
1 teaspoon ground cinnamon
½ teaspoon ground ginger
½ teaspoon nutmeg
1½ cups freshly squeezed orange juice
1½ cups cranberry juice cocktail
2 quarts beer or ale

Fill each cored apple with one teaspoon of the brown sugar and place in a glass baking pan with ¼ inch water. Bake in a preheated 350-degree oven for 30 minutes or until the apples are tender. Combine the remaining ingredients in a stainless-steel pot and heat for 15 minutes without letting the mixture come to a boil. Pour the heated punch into a metal bowl and float the baked apples on top. Serve in heated mugs. Serves 12.

WHITE WINE SANGRÍA

1 bottle dry white wine
1 orange, thinly sliced
2 slices lemon
2 slices lime
1 ounce brandy
2 tablespoons superfine sugar
3-inch stick of cinnamon
10 large strawberries, halved
6 ounces sparkling mineral water

Put all ingredients, except mixer, into a large pitcher and stir to dissolve the sugar. Let flavors marry for at least an hour. Just before serving, add sparkling mineral water and ice cubes to the pitcher and stir gently. Pour into chilled wineglasses. Makes 8 6-ounce drinks.

BRANDY

The hot toddy, a warm and bracing libation when the temperature drops below freezing. Traditionally made with brandy, a hot toddy can also be made with rum, or whiskey.

Brandy falls into two categories—those to be served neat after dinner and those with which cocktails can be made. All the "Star" brandies should be used as mixers. Three Star brandies are fine served on the rocks, with soda, or as a base for a variety of mixed drinks. They are also useful in cooking. Brandies marked V.S.O.P. (Very Superior Old Pale) should never be used for mixed drinks. It is very appropriate, however, to make a mist with a fine, old sipping brandy such as Cognac, Armagnac, or Metaxa.

Perhaps the best known of the brandy cocktails is the Sidecar. It is said to have originated in Paris, where it was named after the motorcycle sidecar occupied by a French Army Captain as he was chauffeured to and from his favorite Parisian watering hole. The drink made its way to the United States, and was instantly taken up by the chic of the speakeasy set.

ALABAMA

1¾ ounces brandy
½ ounce fresh lemon juice
1 teaspoon curaçao
½ teaspoon superfine sugar
1 orange peel

Shake ingredients thoroughly with ice. Strain into a chilled, sugar-rimmed cocktail glass. Twist orange peel over drink and drop into glass.

BALTIMORE BRACER

1 ounce brandy
1 ounce anisette
1 egg white

Shake ingredients vigorously with ice. Strain into a chilled cocktail glass.

BOMBAY

1 ounce brandy
½ ounce dry vermouth
½ ounce sweet vermouth
½ teaspoon curaçao
½ teaspoon Pernod

Shake ingredients thoroughly with ice. Strain into a chilled cocktail glass.

BRANDY ALEXANDER

¾ ounce brandy
¾ ounce crème de cacao
¾ ounce heavy cream
freshly grated nutmeg

Shake ingredients vigorously with ice. Strain into a chilled cocktail glass and dust with freshly grated nutmeg.

BRANDY AND AMER PICON

2 ounces brandy
½ ounce Amer Picon
1 lemon peel and 1 orange peel

Pour ingredients into a mixing glass filled with ice and stir. Strain into an old-fashioned glass filled with ice. Twist peels over drink and drop them into the glass.

BRANDY AND SODA

2 ounces brandy
club soda

Pour ingredients over ice in a highball glass. Stir gently.

BRANDY BEN

1¼ ounces brandy
½ ounce Benedictine
½ ounce fresh orange juice
maraschino cherry

Pour ingredients over ice in an old-fashioned glass and stir gently. Garnish with the maraschino cherry.

BRANDY CASSIS

1½ ounces brandy
1 ounce fresh lemon juice
2 dashes crème de cassis
1 lemon peel

Shake ingredients thoroughly with ice. Strain into a chilled cocktail glass. Twist peel over drink and drop into glass.

BRANDY COLLINS

2 ounces brandy
1 or 2 teaspoons superfine sugar
1 ounce fresh lemon juice
club soda
1 slice of lemon
1 slice of orange
maraschino cherry

Shake all ingredients, except soda, thoroughly with ice. Strain into a collins glass half filled with ice and add club soda. Stir gently. Garnish with fruit slices and cherry.

BRANDY FIZZ

3 ounces brandy
1 tablespoon superfine sugar
2 tablespoons fresh lemon juice
1 tablespoon fresh lime juice
club soda

Shake vigorously all ingredients, except soda, with ice. Strain into a tall glass half filled with ice. Add club soda and stir gently.

BRANDY FLIP

3 ounces brandy
1 whole egg
1 teaspoon superfine sugar
2 teaspoons heavy cream
nutmeg

Shake vigorously first four ingredients with crushed ice. Strain into a Delmonico or sour glass and dust with freshly grated nutmeg.

BRANDY GUMP

2 ounces brandy
½ ounce fresh lemon juice
½ teaspoon grenadine

Shake ingredients well with ice. Strain into a chilled cocktail glass.

BRANDY HIGHBALL

2 ounces brandy
sparkling mineral water or ginger ale
1 lemon peel

Pour brandy over ice in a highball glass. Fill with sparkling mineral water or ginger ale and stir gently. Twist peel over drink and drop into glass.

BRANDY JULEP

5 sprigs fresh mint
1 teaspoon superfine sugar
2½ ounces brandy
slice of orange
maraschino cherry

Fill a tall glass with crushed ice. In a small glass muddle the leaves from two mint sprigs with sugar and a splash of water. Add brandy, stir gently, and strain into the tall glass. Garnish with remaining mint sprigs, the orange slice, and cherry.

BRANDY MANHATTAN

2 ounces brandy
½ ounce sweet vermouth
dash bitters
maraschino cherry

Pour all ingredients into a mixing glass filled with ice and stir. Strain into a cocktail glass and garnish with the cherry.

BRANDY MILK PUNCH

2 ounces brandy
6 ounces chilled whole milk
½ teaspoon superfine sugar
freshly grated nutmeg

Shake well all ingredients, except nutmeg, with ice. Strain into a chilled wine goblet and dust with nutmeg.

BRANDY MINT FIZZ

2 ounces brandy
2 teaspoons white crème de menthe
1 teaspoon crème de cacao
½ ounce fresh lemon juice
½ teaspoon superfine sugar
club soda
1 sprig fresh mint

Shake thoroughly all ingredients, except soda, with ice. Strain into a tall glass half filled with ice and add club soda. Stir gently. Garnish with fresh mint sprig.

BRANDY OLD-FASHIONED

½ teaspoon superfine sugar
2 dashes Angostura bitters
1 teaspoon water
2 ounces brandy
1 lemon peel
1 orange peel
maraschino cherry (optional)

Stir sugar, bitters, and water in an old-fashioned glass until sugar dissolves. Fill the glass with ice, add the brandy, and stir well. Twist peel over drink and drop it into glass. Garnish with the orange slice and cherry.

BRANDY SLING

1 teaspoon superfine sugar
2 tablespoons fresh lemon juice
2 ounces brandy
plain water or sparkling mineral water

Stir sugar and lemon juice in a highball glass until sugar dissolves. Fill the glass with ice, add brandy and mixer, and stir gently.

BRANDY SOUR

2 ounces brandy
½ ounce fresh lemon juice
½ ounce fresh orange juice
½ to 1 teaspoon superfine sugar
half slice of lemon

Shake ingredients thoroughly with ice. Strain into a sour glass and garnish with the half slice of lemon.

BRANDY VERMOUTH COCKTAIL

2 ounces brandy
½ ounce sweet vermouth
dash Angostura bitters

Pour ingredients into a mixing glass filled with ice and stir. Strain into a chilled cocktail glass.

BRANTINI

1½ ounces brandy
1 ounce gin
1 teaspoon dry vermouth
lemon peel

Pour ingredients into a mixing glass filled with ice and stir. Strain into a chilled cocktail glass and twist peel over drink and drop into glass.

CARROL COCKTAIL

1½ ounces brandy
¾ ounce sweet vermouth
maraschino cherry

Pour ingredients into a mixing glass filled with ice and stir. Strain into a chilled cocktail glass and garnish with the cherry.

CHERRY BLOSSOM

1¼ ounces brandy
¾ ounce cherry-flavored brandy
2 teaspoons fresh lemon juice
¼ teaspoon curaçao
¼ teaspoon grenadine

Shake ingredients thoroughly with ice. Strain into a chilled, sugar-rimmed cocktail glass.

DEAUVILLE

1 ounce brandy
½ ounce fresh lemon juice
½ ounce Calvados
½ ounce Triple Sec or Cointreau

Shake all ingredients well with ice. Strain into a chilled cocktail glass.

HOT TODDY

1 sugar cube
2 ounces brandy
lemon peel

Put the sugar cube into an 8-ounce mug, add hot water, and stir until the sugar dissolves. Add the brandy and fill with boiling water. Stir gently. Twist the peel over the drink and drop it into the mug.

JACK ROSE

2 ounces applejack or Calvados
½ ounce fresh lime juice
1 teaspoon grenadine

Shake ingredients well with ice. Strain into a chilled cocktail glass.

LUGGER

1 ounce brandy
1 ounce applejack or Calvados
1 dash apricot-flavored brandy

Shake ingredients well with ice and strain into a chilled cocktail glass.

MIKADO

1 ounce brandy
1 dash Triple Sec
1 dash grenadine
1 dash Crème de noyau
1 dash Angostura bitters

Pour ingredients into an old-fashioned glass filled with ice and stir.

PHOEBE SNOW

1¼ ounces brandy
1¼ ounces Dubonnet
½ teaspoon Pernod

Shake ingredients well with ice. Strain into a chilled cocktail glass.

PIMM'S CUP NO. 1

1½ ounces Pimm's No. 1
lemon soda
1 slice lemon
cucumber peel
cucumber stick

Pour Pimm's No. 1 over ice in a tall glass and fill with lemon soda. Add lemon slice and cucumber peel and stir. Garnish with the cucumber stick.

POLONAISE

1½ ounces brandy
½ ounce blackberry brandy
½ ounce dry sherry
1 teaspoon fresh lemon juice
2 dashes of orange bitters

Shake all ingredients thoroughly with ice and strain into an old-fashioned glass filled with ice.

SIDECAR

1½ ounces brandy
½ ounce Cointreau
½ ounce fresh lemon juice

Shake ingredients well with ice. Strain into a chilled cocktail glass.

STINGER

1½ ounces brandy
½ ounce white crème de menthe

Shake ingredients well with ice and strain into a chilled cocktail glass.

GIN

A dramatic presentation for that classic gin drink, the Martini.

Despite the evil reputation so rightfully earned by gin in the eighteenth century, this colorless, juniper-flavored liquid has more than managed to live it down. Once the scourge of the British Empire, gin has climbed the ladder of respectability with such inventions as the Martini, the Gimlet, and the Ramos Gin Fizz. Henry C. Ramos owes his immortality to his thirst-quenching concoction, originally mixed in his New Orleans bar in the 1880s. The secrets of the Ramos Gin Fizz's delightful taste, texture, and aroma are vigorous shaking, orange-flower water, and egg whites. A purist, Mr. Ramos reportedly hired a staff of young boys to shake the fizzes for a full five minutes before he allowed them to be poured for his waiting customers.

ANGEL FACE

1 ounce gin
½ ounce apricot brandy
½ ounce applejack or Calvados

Shake all ingredients well with ice and strain into a cocktail glass.

BENNETT COCKTAIL

1½ ounces gin
½ ounce freshly squeezed lime juice
½ teaspoon superfine sugar
2 dashes Angostura bitters
lime peel

Shake all ingredients thoroughly with ice and strain into a chilled cocktail glass. Twist lime peel over drink and drop into glass.

BLOODHOUND

½ ounce dry vermouth
½ ounce sweet vermouth
1 ounce gin
2 fresh strawberries

Shake all ingredients well with ice. Strain into a cocktail glass and garnish with fresh strawberries.

BLUE DEVIL

1½ ounces gin
½ ounce blue curaçao
½ ounce fresh lemon juice
1 slice of lemon

Shake all ingredients well with ice. Strain into a cocktail glass and garnish with the lemon slice.

BLUE MOON

1½ ounces gin
¾ ounce Crème Yvette
lemon peel

Pour ingredients into a mixing glass filled with ice and stir. Strain into a chilled cocktail glass. Twist lemon peel over drink and drop it into the glass.

BRONX

1½ ounces gin
½ ounce fresh orange juice
¼ ounce dry vermouth
¼ ounce sweet vermouth

Shake all ingredients well with ice. Strain into a chilled cocktail glass.

CABARET

1½ ounces gin
½ teaspoon dry vermouth
¼ teaspoon Benedictine
2 dashes Angostura bitters
maraschino cherry

Pour all ingredients into a mixing glass filled with ice and stir. Strain into a cocktail glass and garnish with the cherry.

CLOVER CLUB

1½ ounces gin
¾ ounce freshly squeezed lemon
    juice
1 teaspoon grenadine
half an egg white

Shake all ingredients vigorously and strain into a chilled cocktail glass.

COLONIAL

1½ ounces gin
½ ounce grapefruit juice
1 teaspoon maraschino

Shake all ingredients well with ice. Strain into a chilled cocktail glass.

COPENHAGEN

1 ounce gin
1 ounce aquavit
¼ ounce dry vermouth
green olive

Pour all ingredients into a mixing glass filled with ice and stir. Strain into a cocktail glass and garnish with the olive.

CRYSTAL SLIPPER

¾ ounce gin
¾ ounce Crème Yvette
2 dashes bitters

Pour all ingredients into a mixing glass filled with ice and stir. Strain into a cocktail glass.

DELMONICO

1½ ounces gin
1 ounce dry vermouth
1 dash orange bitters
lemon peel

Pour ingredients into a mixing glass filled with ice and stir gently. Strain into a chilled cocktail glass. Twist lemon peel over drink and drop into glass.

DEMPSEY

1½ ounces gin
1 ounce Calvados or applejack
2 dashes Pernod
2 dashes grenadine

Pour all ingredients into a mixing glass filled with ice and stir. Strain into a cocktail glass.

DIAMOND FIZZ

2 ounces gin
juice of half a lemon
1 teaspoon superfine sugar
4 to 6 ounces chilled brut champagne

Shake well all ingredients, except champagne, with ice. Strain into a highball glass half filled with ice, add champagne, and stir gently.

DIXIE

¾ ounce gin
½ ounce Pernod
½ ounce dry vermouth
2 dashes grenadine
2 tablespoons freshly squeezed orange juice

Shake all ingredients well with ice. Strain into a cocktail glass.

DUBONNET COCKTAIL

1½ ounces gin
1½ ounces Dubonnet
1 dash orange bitters (optional)
lemon peel

Pour all ingredients into a mixing glass filled with ice and stir. Strain into a cocktail glass, and twist peel over drink and drop it into glass.

EMERALD COOLER

1 ounce gin
½ ounce green crème de menthe
1 ounce sweetened lemon juice
club soda
lemon peel

Pour all ingredients, except mixer, over ice in a highball glass. Fill the glass with club soda and stir gently. Twist lemon peel over drink and drop it into the glass.

FRANKENJACK

1 ounce gin
1 ounce dry vermouth
½ ounce apricot brandy
½ ounce Cointreau
maraschino cherry

Pour all ingredients into a mixing glass filled with ice and stir. Strain into a cocktail glass and garnish with the cherry.

FRENCH 75

1½ ounces gin
juice of half a lemon
½ teaspoon superfine sugar
chilled brut champagne

Shake well all ingredients, except champagne, with cracked ice. Do not strain. Pour ice and mixture into a highball glass and fill with champagne. Stir gently.

GIBSON

¼ ounce dry vermouth
2½ ounces gin
cocktail onion

Pour vermouth over ice in a mixing glass. Add gin and stir gently until well chilled. Strain into a chilled cocktail glass and garnish with an onion.

GIMLET

2½ ounces gin
½ ounce Rose's lime juice

Pour ingredients into a mixing glass filled with ice and stir well. Strain into a chilled cocktail glass.

GIN ALOHA

1½ ounces gin
1½ teaspoons Triple Sec
1 tablespoon unsweetened pineapple juice
1 dash orange bitters

Shake all ingredients thoroughly with ice and strain into a chilled cocktail glass.

GIN BUCK

1½ ounces gin
juice of half a lemon
ginger ale

Pour ingredients into a highball glass filled with ice. Add ginger ale and stir gently.

GIN CASSIS

1½ ounces gin
½ ounce fresh lemon juice
½ ounce crème de cassis

Shake ingredients well with ice. Pour into an old-fashioned glass half filled with ice.

GIN AND CIN

2 ounces gin
1 ounce Cinzano

Pour ingredients into a cocktail glass and stir. No ice is used in this drink.

GIN AND LIME COCKTAIL

1½ ounces gin
½ ounce freshly squeezed lime juice
½ ounce freshly squeezed orange
  juice
1 teaspoon Rose's lime juice
lime peel

Shake ingredients well with ice and strain into a chilled cocktail glass. Twist lime peel over drink and drop it into the glass.

GIN AND TONIC

wedge of lime
1½ ounces gin
quinine water

Squeeze lime over ice in a highball glass and drop the shell into the glass. Pour in gin and fill the glass with quinine water. Stir gently.

GIN DAIQUIRI

1½ ounces gin
½ ounce light rum
½ ounce freshly squeezed lime juice
1 teaspoon superfine sugar

Shake ingredients well with ice and strain into a chilled cocktail glass.

GIN FIZZ

2 ounces gin
1 tablespoon superfine sugar
1 ounce fresh lemon juice
1 ounce fresh lime juice
club soda

Shake thoroughly all ingredients, except mixer, with ice. Strain into a highball glass filled with ice and add club soda.

GIN HIGHBALL

2 ounces gin
sparkling mineral water or ginger ale
lemon peel

Pour gin over ice into a highball glass, add mixer, and stir gently. Twist peel over drink and drop into glass.

GIN RICKEY

juice of half a lime
1½ ounces gin
sparkling mineral water

Squeeze lime over ice in a tall glass and drop the shell into the glass. Pour in gin and fill the glass with sparkling mineral water. Stir gently.

GIN SLING

1 teaspoon superfine sugar
2 tablespoons fresh lemon juice
2 ounces gin
plain water or sparkling mineral
  water

Stir sugar and lemon juice in a highball glass until sugar dissolves. Fill the glass with ice, add gin and mixer, and stir gently.

GIN SOUR

2 ounces gin
2 ounces fresh lemon juice
1 tablespoon superfine sugar
1 slice of orange or lemon
maraschino cherry

Shake all ingredients well with ice. Strain into a chilled sour glass and garnish with the fruit.

GOLDEN FIZZ

1½ ounces gin
1 tablespoon superfine sugar
2 tablespoons fresh lemon juice
1 tablespoon fresh lime juice
1 egg yolk
club soda

Shake well all ingredients, except mixer, with ice. Strain into a highball glass filled with ice and add club soda.

MAGNOLIA

3 ounces gin
1 ounce heavy cream
2 tablespoons fresh lemon juice
½ teaspoon grenadine

Shake all ingredients very well with ice. Strain into a cocktail glass.

MARTINI

½ ounce dry vermouth
2 ounces gin
1 lemon peel or green olive

Pour vermouth over ice in a mixing glass. Add gin and stir gently until well chilled. Strain into a cocktail glass and garnish with the green olive or lemon peel. If lemon garnish is preferred, twist the peel over the drink, rub the rim of the glass with it, and drop it into the glass.

This classic gin drink, thought to have been first prepared in San Francisco in the late nineteenth century, can also be made with rum, tequila, or vodka.

MARTINI (DRY)

⅓ ounce dry vermouth
2 ounces gin
1 lemon peel or green olive

Follow the procedure for preparing a martini.

MARTINI (EXTRA DRY)

¼ ounce dry vermouth
2 ounces gin
1 lemon peel or green olive

Follow the procedure for preparing a martini.

MERRY WIDOW

1¼ ounces gin
1¼ ounces dry vermouth
½ teaspoon Benedictine
½ teaspoon anisette
1 dash orange bitters
1 lemon peel

Pour all ingredients into a mixing glass filled with ice and stir. Strain into a cocktail glass and garnish with the lemon peel.

MORRO

1 ounce gin
½ ounce golden rum
1 tablespoon pineapple juice
1 tablespoon freshly squeezed lime juice
½ teaspoon superfine sugar

Shake ingredients thoroughly with ice and strain into a chilled cocktail glass.

ORANGE BLOSSOM

1½ ounces gin
1 ounce freshly squeezed orange juice
1 slice of orange

Shake ingredients well with ice. Strain into a sugar-frosted cocktail glass and garnish with the orange slice.

ORANGE BUCK

1½ ounces gin
1 ounce freshly squeezed orange juice
½ ounce fresh lemon juice
ginger ale
1 slice of orange

Shake well all ingredients, except mixer, with ice. Strain into a highball glass half filled with ice and add ginger ale. Stir gently. Garnish with the orange slice.

PARK AVENUE

1½ ounces gin
¾ ounce sweet vermouth
1 tablespoon pineapple juice

Pour all ingredients into a mixing glass filled with ice and stir. Strain into a chilled cocktail glass.

PERFECT

1½ ounces gin
½ ounce dry vermouth
½ ounce sweet vermouth
1 lemon peel

Pour ingredients into a mixing glass filled with ice and stir. Strain into a chilled cocktail glass, and twist peel over drink and drop it into glass.

PERNOD MARTINI

½ ounce Pernod
2 ounces gin
½ ounce dry vermouth

Swirl Pernod around in a prechilled cocktail glass until the inside is completely coated. Discard excess. Pour remaining ingredients into a mixing glass filled with ice and stir. Strain into the coated glass.

PINK GIN

2½ ounces gin
1 dash Angostura bitters

Pour ingredients into a mixing glass filled with ice and stir. Strain into a cocktail glass.

PINK LADY

1½ ounces gin
¼ ounce fresh lime juice
1 teaspoon heavy cream
1 teaspoon grenadine
½ egg white

Shake ingredients vigorously with ice. Strain into a chilled cocktail glass.

PRINCETON

1¼ ounces gin
¾ ounce dry vermouth
½ ounce freshly squeezed lime juice

Pour all ingredients into a mixing glass filled with ice and stir. Strain into a chilled cocktail glass.

RAMOS GIN FIZZ

juice of half a lemon
juice of half a lime
1 egg white
1 tablespoon heavy cream
1 teaspoon superfine sugar
1½ ounces gin
½ teaspoon orange-flower water
sparkling mineral water

Shake vigorously all ingredients, except mixer, with ice. Strain into a highball glass over three ice cubes and fill with sparkling mineral water.

RENAISSANCE

1½ ounces gin
½ ounce dry sherry
1 tablespoon heavy cream
freshly grated nutmeg

Shake ingredients thoroughly with ice and strain into a chilled cocktail glass. Dust with the nutmeg.

ROYAL GIN FIZZ

2 ounces gin
2 tablespoons fresh lemon juice
1 teaspoon superfine sugar
1 whole egg
club soda

Shake vigorously all ingredients, except mixer, with ice. Strain into a highball glass over three ice cubes and fill with soda.

SAN SEBASTIAN

1 ounce gin
¼ ounce rum
½ ounce grapefruit juice
½ ounce curaçao
½ ounce fresh lemon juice

Shake all ingredients well with ice and strain into a chilled cocktail glass.

SILVER FIZZ

3 ounces gin
1 tablespoon superfine sugar
2 tablespoons fresh lemon juice
1 tablespoon fresh lime juice
1 egg white
club soda

Shake vigorously all ingredients, except mixer, with ice. Strain into a highball glass over three ice cubes and fill with soda.

SINGAPORE SLING

1½ ounces gin
1 ounce cherry brandy
2½ ounces fresh lime juice
1 teaspoon superfine sugar
club soda
1 slice of lime

Shake vigorously first four ingredients in a cocktail shaker half filled with ice. Strain into a tall glass half filled with ice cubes and add soda. Garnish with the slice of lime.

SLOE GIN FIZZ

1 ounce sloe gin
1 ounce gin
¾ ounce fresh lemon juice
½ teaspoon superfine sugar
club soda
1 slice of lemon

Shake thoroughly first four ingredients, except mixer, with ice. Strain into a tall glass half filled with ice cubes and add soda. Garnish with the slice of lemon.

SNOWBALL

1 ounce gin
¼ ounce crème de violette
¼ ounce white crème de menthe
¼ ounce anisette
1 ounce heavy cream

Shake all ingredients vigorously with ice. Strain into a chilled cocktail glass.

SPINNAKER

¾ ounce gin
¾ ounce Benedictine
4 ounces freshly squeezed orange
   juice
1 orange peel

Shake ingredients well with ice. Strain into an ice-filled old-fashioned glass. Twist peel over drink and drop it into glass.

TOM COLLINS

1½ ounces gin
1 or 2 teaspoons superfine sugar
3 ounces fresh lemon juice
club soda
1 slice each of lemon and orange
1 maraschino cherry

Shake thoroughly all ingredients, except soda, with ice. Strain into a collins glass half filled with ice and add club soda. Stir gently. Garnish with the fruit.

WHITE LADY

2 ounces gin
1 ounce Cointreau or Triple Sec
½ ounce fresh lemon juice

Shake all ingredients well with ice. Strain into a chilled cocktail glass.

RUM

Named by its inventor after a Cuban mining town, the Daiquiri is one of today's most popular rum drinks, having spawned numerous delightful variations.

Rum, a sugar-based spirit, is the toast of the Caribbean islands, and the base for such world-renowned drinks as the Daiquiri, Planter's Punch, the Cuba Libre, and the Piña Colada (which literally means "strained pineapple"). Piña Coladas were first mixed in 1958 at the beach bar of the Caribe Hilton in San Juan, Puerto Rico, by Ramon Marrero. Over the last twenty years, Mr. Marrero has personally shaken over 3 million Coladas, a testament to the popularity of this heady mixture of rum, pineapple, and coconut cream, and to this gentleman's staying power.

ACAPULCO

1½ ounces light rum
½ ounce freshly squeezed lime juice
¼ ounce Triple Sec
½ egg white
½ teaspoon superfine sugar
fresh mint leaves

Shake all ingredients thoroughly with ice. Strain into a chilled cocktail glass and garnish with mint leaves.

BANANA DAIQUIRI

1½ ounces light rum
½ ounce banana liqueur (optional)
½ ounce fresh lime juice
½ small, ripe banana, sliced

Put all ingredients into an electric blender. Add one-half cup of crushed ice and blend at high speed until smooth. Pour into a saucer champagne glass or a wine goblet.

BACARDI

1½ ounces light or golden Bacardi rum
½ ounce fresh lime juice
1 teaspoon grenadine

Shake ingredients well with ice. Strain into a chilled cocktail glass.

BACARDI SPECIAL

1½ ounces light rum
¾ ounce gin
1½ tablespoons fresh lime juice
1 teaspoon grenadine

Shake ingredients vigorously with ice. Strain into a chilled cocktail glass.

BEACHCOMBER

1½ ounces light rum
½ ounce dry vermouth
½ ounce sweet vermouth

Pour ingredients into a mixing glass filled with ice and stir. Strain into a chilled cocktail glass.

BEE'S KNEES

1½ ounces light rum
2 ounces freshly squeezed orange juice
½ ounce fresh lime juice
1 teaspoon superfine sugar
2 dashes orange bitters
1 orange peel

Shake all ingredients well with ice. Strain into a chilled cocktail glass, twist peel over drink, and drop it into glass.

BLACK DEVIL

2½ ounces light rum
½ ounce dry vermouth
1 black olive

Pour ingredients into a mixing glass filled with ice and stir. Strain into a cocktail glass and garnish with the black olive.

BLUEBEARD'S WENCH

1½ ounces light rum
1½ ounces Cointreau or Triple Sec
1½ ounces blue curaçao
¾ ounce fresh lemon juice
club soda or sparkling mineral water
maraschino cherry

Shake thoroughly all ingredients, except mixer, with ice. Strain into a tall glass filled with ice, add mixer and garnish with the cherry.

BOLO

1½ ounces light rum
1 ounce fresh lime juice
1 ounce freshly squeezed orange juice
1 tablespoon superfine sugar

Shake ingredients vigorously with ice. Strain into a chilled cocktail glass.

CARIBE

1 ounce light rum
1 ounce gin
½ ounce fresh lime juice
1 teaspoon superfine sugar
1 slice of orange

Shake all ingredients well with ice Strain into an old-fashioned glass filled with ice. Garnish with the orange slice.

CASA BLANCA

2 ounces golden rum
1 dash Angostura bitters
1 teaspoon freshly squeezed lime juice
¼ teaspoon curaçao
¼ teaspoon maraschino

Shake all ingredients thoroughly with ice. Strain into a chilled cocktail glass.

CONTINENTAL

1¾ ounces light rum
½ ounce freshly squeezed lime juice
½ teaspoon superfine sugar
½ teaspoon green crème de menthe

Shake ingredients well with ice and strain into a chilled cocktail glass.

CORKSCREW

1½ ounces light rum
½ ounce dry vermouth
½ ounce peach brandy
1 slice lime

Shake all ingredients well with ice and strain into a chilled cocktail glass. Garnish with the slice of lime.

CUBA LIBRE

juice of ½ lime
2 ounces light rum
cola

Squeeze lime over ice in a highball glass and drop the shell into the glass. Pour in rum and fill the glass with cola. Stir gently.

DAIQUIRI

2 ounces light rum
2½ ounces fresh lime juice
½ tablespoon superfine sugar (or to taste)

Shake all ingredients well with ice. Strain into a chilled cocktail glass or into an old-fashioned glass filled with ice.

DERBY DAIQUIRI

1½ ounces light rum
2 ounces freshly squeezed orange juice
1½ ounces fresh lime juice
1 tablespoon superfine sugar

Put all ingredients into an electric blender. Add one third cup of crushed ice and blend at high speed until smooth. Pour into a saucer champagne glass or a wine goblet.

DEVIL'S TAIL

1 ounce golden rum
¾ ounce vodka
2½ ounces fresh lime juice
¼ ounce grenadine
¼ ounce apricot-flavored brandy
1 lime peel

Put all ingredients into an electric blender. Add one half cup of crushed ice and blend at low speed. Pour into a saucer champagne glass. Twist peel over drink and drop it into glass.

EL PRESIDENTE

1½ ounces light rum
½ ounce white curaçao
½ ounce dry vermouth
1 dash grenadine

Shake all ingredients vigorously with ice. Strain into a chilled cocktail glass.

FAIR AND WARMER

1½ ounces rum
¾ ounce sweet vermouth
½ teaspoon Triple Sec

Pour ingredients into a mixing glass filled with ice and stir. Strain into a chilled cocktail glass.

FROZEN DAIQUIRI

2 ounces light rum
2½ ounces fresh lime juice
½ tablespoon superfine sugar (or to taste)

Put all ingredients into an electric blender. Add one-half cup of crushed ice and blend at high speed until smooth. Pour into a saucer champagne glass or a wine goblet.

FROZEN PASSION FRUIT DAIQUIRI

1½ ounces light rum
½ ounce passion fruit syrup
½ ounce freshly squeezed lime juice
½ ounce freshly squeezed orange juice
¼ ounce freshly squeezed lemon juice

Put all ingredients into an electric blender. Add one-third cup of crushed ice and blend at low speed until smooth. Pour into a saucer champagne glass.

FROZEN PEACH DAIQUIRI

1½ ounces light rum
½ ounce fresh lime juice
¼ cup frozen peaches, thawed
1 tablespoon peach syrup

Thaw peaches and reserve the syrup. Put all ingredients into an electric blender. Add one third cup of crushed ice and blend at low speed until smooth. Pour into a saucer champagne glass.

FROZEN PINEAPPLE DAIQUIRI

1½ ounces light rum
½ ounce fresh lime juice
½ teaspoon sugar
4 pineapple chunks, canned without sugar

Put all ingredients into an electric blender. Add one third cup of crushed ice and blend at low speed until smooth. Pour into a saucer champagne glass.

FROZEN STRAWBERRY DAIQUIRI

1½ ounces light rum
½ ounce strawberry liqueur
½ cup sliced fresh strawberries
½ ounce fresh lemon juice
1 teaspoon superfine sugar
1 fresh strawberry with stem
   attached

Put all ingredients into an electric blender. Add one third cup of crushed ice and blend at low speed until smooth. Pour into a saucer champagne glass or a wine goblet. Garnish with the fresh strawberry.

GAUGUIN

2 ounces light rum
½ ounce passion fruit syrup
½ ounce freshly squeezed lemon
   juice
¼ ounce freshly squeezed lime juice
maraschino cherry

Put all ingredients into an electric blender. Add one-third cup of crushed ice and blend at low speed until smooth. Pour into a saucer champagne glass. Garnish with the maraschino cherry.

GROG

2 ounces dark rum
1 sugar cube
3 whole cloves
1-inch piece of cinnamon stick
1 tablespoon fresh lemon juice

Put all ingredients into an 8-ounce mug and stir until the sugar is dissolved. Fill the mug with boiling water and stir again.

HOT BUTTERED RUM

2 ounces dark rum
½ teaspoon superfine sugar (or to
   taste)
1 lemon peel
1 cinnamon stick
2 whole cloves
water or apple cider
1 teaspoon sweet butter
nutmeg

Put the rum, sugar, lemon peel, and spices in a mug. Bring the water or cider just to the boiling point and pour it into the spiced rum mixture. Add the butter and stir well. Dust with freshly grated nutmeg.

HOT RUM AND CHOCOLATE

6 ounces hot chocolate
1½ ounces light rum
whipped cream
freshly grated orange rind
cocoa

Fill a mug two thirds full with hot chocolate, add rum, and stir gently. Top with whipped cream and sprinkle on the orange rind. Lightly dust with the cocoa.

HURRICANE

1 ounce dark Jamaican rum
1 ounce light rum
1 tablespoon passion fruit syrup
2 teaspoons fresh lime juice

Shake ingredients thoroughly with ice and strain into a chilled cocktail glass.

MAI TAI

2 ounces light rum
2½ ounces fresh lime juice
¼ teaspoon Triple Sec
¼ teaspoon orgeat
1 tablespoon superfine sugar
1 sprig fresh mint
1 slice of lime
1 pineapple stick

Shake ingredients well with ice. Strain into a tall glass and fill it with cracked ice. Garnish with the mint and fruit.

MARTINIQUE

¾ ounce light rum
¾ ounce Benedictine
4 ounces pineapple juice
1 spear fresh pineapple

Shake ingredients thoroughly with ice. Strain over ice into an old-fashioned glass. Garnish with the pineapple spear.

MONKEY'S PAW

1½ ounces dark Jamaican rum
3 ounces unsweetened pineapple
   juice
sparkling mineral water

Pour ingredients over ice in a tall glass and stir gently.

MONKEY WRENCH

1½ ounces light rum
grapefruit juice

Pour rum over ice in a tall glass. Fill with grapefruit juice and stir gently.

This smooth blend of rum, coconut, and pineapple juice, the Piña Colada, is a warm weather refresher anywhere in the world whenever the temperature begins to soar.

PIÑA COLADA

1½ ounces light or dark rum
1 ounce cream of coconut
3 ounces unsweetened pineapple juice
1 spear pineapple
maraschino cherry

Put all ingredients into an electric blender. Add one half cup of crushed ice and blend at low speed until smooth. Pour into a tall glass or large goblet half filled with ice. Garnish with the fruit.

PINK VERANDA

1½ ounces light or golden rum
2½ ounces cranberry juice cocktail
½ ounce fresh lime juice
1 teaspoon superfine sugar
½ egg white
1 slice of orange
1 fresh strawberry

Shake all ingredients thoroughly with ice. Strain into an old-fashioned glass and fill with ice cubes. Garnish with the orange slice and the strawberry.

PLANTER'S PUNCH

1 tablespoon fresh lime juice
2 tablespoons fresh lemon juice
3 ounces freshly squeezed orange juice
1 ounce light rum
1½ ounces dark rum
½ ounce grenadine
2 dashes Triple Sec
1 slice each of lemon and orange
1 pineapple spear
mint sprig dipped in superfine sugar

Fill a collins glass two thirds full with crushed ice. Add the fruit juices and light rum and stir gently until the glass is frosted. Add the dark rum and stir again. Top with the Triple Sec and garnish with the fruit and mint.

RUM AND SODA

1½ ounces light or golden rum
club soda
1 slice of lemon or lime

Pour rum over ice in a highball glass. Fill with the club soda and stir gently. Garnish with the lemon or lime.

RUM AND TONIC

1½ ounces light rum
quinine water
1 slice of lime

Pour rum over ice in a highball glass. Fill with quinine water and stir gently. Garnish with lime.

RUM BLOODY MARY

1½ ounces light rum
4½ ounces tomato juice
squeeze of fresh lemon (to taste)
dash of Worcestershire sauce
dash of Tabasco sauce
salt and pepper to taste
rib of celery

Shake ingredients well with ice. Strain into a chilled glass or pour over ice cubes. Garnish with celery.

RUM COLLINS

2½ ounces fresh lemon juice
1 tablespoon superfine sugar
1½ ounces light rum
club soda
1 slice each of lemon and orange
maraschino cherry

Shake all ingredients, except the soda, thoroughly with ice. Strain into a collins glass half filled with ice, and add soda. Stir gently. Garnish with fruit.

RUM DUBONNET

1½ ounces light rum
¾ ounce Dubonnet
1 teaspoon fresh lime juice
1 lime peel

Shake ingredients well with ice. Strain into a chilled cocktail glass and twist peel over drink and drop it into the glass.

RUM GIMLET

2½ ounces light rum
½ ounce Rose's lime juice

Pour ingredients into a mixing glass filled with ice and stir well. Strain into a chilled cocktail glass.

RUM HIGHBALL

1½ ounces light rum
sparkling mineral water
1 lemon peel

Pour rum over ice in a highball glass. Fill with sparkling mineral water and stir gently. Twist lemon peel over drink and drop into glass.

RUM MARTINI

½ ounce dry vermouth
2½ ounces light rum
1 lemon peel

Pour vermouth over ice in a mixing glass. Add rum and stir gently until well chilled. Strain into a cocktail glass, twist the peel over the drink, rub the rim of the glass with it, and drop it into the glass.

RUM SCREWDRIVER

1½ ounces light rum
3 ounces freshly squeezed orange juice
1 slice of orange

Pour rum and orange juice over ice in an old-fashioned glass and stir until mixed. Garnish with the orange slice.

RUM SOUR

1½ ounces light rum
2½ ounces fresh lemon juice
1 tablespoon superfine sugar
1 orange slice
maraschino cherry

Shake all ingredients thoroughly with ice and strain into a sour glass. Garnish with the orange slice and cherry.

SCORPION

2 ounces light rum
2 ounces freshly squeezed orange juice
1½ ounces fresh lemon juice
1 ounce brandy
½ ounce orgeat
1 slice of orange

Put all ingredients into an electric blender. Add one third cup of crushed ice and blend at low speed until smooth. Pour into a highball glass and fill with ice cubes. Garnish with the orange slice.

SUNDOWNER

¾ ounce light rum
¾ ounce Benedictine
4 ounces freshly squeezed orange juice
1 slice of orange
maraschino cherry

Shake ingredients well with ice. Strain into a tall glass, add ice cubes, and garnish with the fruit.

ZOMBIE

¾ ounce 90-proof rum
1½ ounces golden rum
¾ ounce light rum
¾ ounce pineapple juice
¾ ounce papaya juice
3 tablespoons fresh lime juice
1 teaspoon superfine sugar
1 pineapple stick
1 maraschino cherry
1 tablespoon Demerara rum

Shake thoroughly all ingredients, except Demerara rum, with ice. Strain into a highball glass and add ice cubes. Garnish with the fruit and float the Demerara rum on top.

TEQUILA

Photograph by Don Kushnick

This satisfyingly tart tequila-based speciality, the Margarita, is presented at its classical best — in a long-stemmed cocktail glass, its rim frosted with salt.

Tequila is Mexico's contribution to the world of spirits and is often called "cactus whiskey." A fiery liquid derived from the fruitlike maguey cactus, the process of its distillation is similar to that used for grapes and apples. Although tequila was once considered an acquired taste, by now it has been acquired by many people. The dramatic rise of the Margarita, the Tequila Sunrise, and the Bloody María attest to the liquid's newly won popularity. Many aficionados, however, still believe there is only one way to down the liquid — in a Tequila Shooter.

BLOODY MARÍA

1½ ounces tequila
3 ounces tomato juice
1 teaspoon fresh lemon juice
1 dash Tabasco sauce
1 dash celery salt
1 slice of lemon

Shake all ingredients well with ice. Strain into an old-fashioned glass and add ice cubes. Garnish with the lemon slice.

CHAPALA

1½ ounces tequila
2 ounces freshly squeezed orange juice
½ ounce lemon juice
1 dash orange-flower water
2 teaspoons grenadine
1 slice of orange

Shake all ingredients well with ice. Strain into an old-fashioned glass filled with ice. Garnish with the orange slice.

EL DIABLO

1½ ounces tequila
½ ounce crème de cassis
1½ teaspoons fresh lime juice
sparkling mineral water
1 slice of lime

Pour ingredients over ice in a tall glass. Add sparkling mineral water and stir gently. Garnish with the slice of lime.

FROZEN BLACKBERRY TEQUILA

1½ ounces tequila
1 ounce blackberry liqueur
½ ounce fresh lemon juice
1 slice lemon

Put all ingredients into an electric blender. Add one third cup crushed ice and blend at low speed until smooth. Pour into an old-fashioned glass and add ice cubes. Garnish with the slice of lemon.

FROZEN MATADOR

1½ ounces tequila
2 ounces pineapple juice
½ ounce fresh lime juice
1 stick pineapple

Put all ingredients into an electric blender. Add one third cup of crushed ice and blend at low speed until smooth. Pour into a saucer champagne glass and garnish with the pineapple stick.

FROZEN TEQUILA SCREWDRIVER

1½ ounces tequila
3 ounces freshly squeezed orange juice
1 slice of orange

Put all ingredients into an electric blender. Add one third cup of crushed ice and blend at low speed until smooth. Pour into a saucer champagne glass and garnish with the orange slice.

GENTLE BEN

¾ ounce tequila
¾ ounce gin
¾ ounce vodka
freshly squeezed orange juice
1 slice of orange
maraschino cherry

Pour ingredients, except orange juice, into a mixing glass filled with ice and stir. Strain into a collins glass over ice cubes and add orange juice. Stir gently to mix. Garnish with the fruit.

MARGARITA

1½ ounces tequila
½ ounce Triple Sec or Cointreau
½ ounce fresh lime juice
1 lime peel (optional)

Shake all ingredients well with ice. Strain into a chilled, salt-rimmed cocktail glass. Twist lime peel over drink and drop it into glass.

MATADOR

1½ ounces tequila
2 ounces pineapple juice
½ ounce fresh lime juice
1 slice of lime

Shake all ingredients thoroughly. Strain into an old-fashioned glass and add ice cubes. Garnish with the lime.

MEXICANA

1½ ounces tequila
1 ounce fresh lemon juice
1 ounce pineapple juice
1 teaspoon grenadine

Shake all ingredients well with ice and strain into a chilled cocktail glass.

MEXICOLA

juice of ½ lime
2 ounces tequila
cola

Squeeze lime over ice in a highball glass and drop the shell into the glass. Pour in tequila and fill the glass with cola. Stir gently.

PICADOR

2 ounces tequila
1 ounce Kahlúa
1 lemon peel

Pour ingredients into a mixing glass filled with crushed ice and stir. Strain into a cocktail glass, twist peel over drink, and drop it into the glass.

PRADO

1½ ounces tequila
¾ ounce fresh lime juice
½ egg white
½ ounce maraschino
1 teaspoon grenadine
½ slice of lemon
maraschino cherry

Shake ingredients thoroughly with ice. Strain into a chilled sour glass and garnish with the fruit.

SLOE TEQUILA

1 ounce tequila
½ ounce sloe gin
½ ounce fresh lime juice
cucumber peel

Pour all ingredients into an electric blender. Add one third cup of crushed ice and blend at low speed until smooth. Pour into an old-fashioned glass and add ice cubes. Garnish with the cucumber peel.

SOMBRERO MEXICALI

¾ ounce tequila
¾ ounce coffee-flavored brandy
1 ounce heavy cream

Pour ingredients over ice in an old-fashioned glass and stir gently.

STRAWBERRY MARGARITA

1½ ounces tequila
½ ounce strawberry liqueur
½ cup sliced fresh strawberries
½ ounce fresh lime juice
½ teaspoon superfine sugar
1 fresh strawberry with stem attached

Put all ingredients into an electric blender. Add one third cup crushed ice and blend at low speed until smooth. Pour into a saucer champagne glass and garnish with the fruit.

TEQUILA AND TEA

1½ ounces tequila
iced tea
superfine sugar
lemon wedge

Pour tequila over ice in a highball glass. Pour in iced tea and add sugar and lemon to taste.

TEQUILA AND TONIC

1½ ounces tequila
wedge of lime
tonic water

Pour tequila over ice in a highball glass. Squeeze lime and drop the shell into the glass. Add tonic water and stir gently.

TEQUILA COLADA

1½ ounces tequila
1 ounce cream of coconut
3 ounces unsweetened pineapple juice
1 pineapple stick
1 slice of lime
maraschino cherry

Put all ingredients into an electric blender. Add one half cup of crushed ice and blend at low speed until smooth. Pour into a tall glass or large goblet half filled with ice. Garnish with the pineapple stick, the lime slice, and the maraschino cherry.

TEQUILA COLLINS

1½ ounces tequila
1 tablespoon superfine sugar
2½ ounces fresh lime juice
club soda
1 slice of lime
1 slice of orange
maraschino cherry

Shake all ingredients, except soda, thoroughly with ice. Strain into a collins glass half filled with ice and add club soda. Stir gently. Garnish with fruit slices and cherry.

TEQUILA DRIVER

1½ ounces tequila
freshly squeezed orange juice
1 dash of orange-flower water
1 slice of orange

Pour tequila over ice in a highball glass. Add freshly squeezed orange juice and stir gently. Sprinkle the top of the drink with orange-flower water and garnish with the orange slice.

TEQUILA DUBONNET

1½ ounces tequila
1½ ounces Dubonnet
1 slice of lemon

Pour ingredients over ice in an old-fashioned glass. Stir gently. Garnish with the lemon slice.

TEQUILA GIMLET

2½ ounces tequila
½ ounce Rose's lime juice

Pour ingredients into a mixing glass filled with ice and stir well. Strain into a chilled cocktail glass.

TEQUILA MOCKINGBIRD

2½ ounces tequila
½ ounce dry vermouth
1 small, pitted black olive

Pour ingredients into a mixing glass filled with ice and stir until well chilled. Strain into a chilled cocktail glass and garnish with the olive.

TEQUILA PINK

1½ ounces tequila
1 ounce dry vermouth
1 dash grenadine

Shake all ingredients well with ice and strain into a chilled cocktail glass.

TEQUILA SHOOTER

1 ounce tequila
salt
1 wedge of lemon or lime

Pour tequila into a shot glass. Put salt in hand, lick salt, swallow tequila, and bite into lemon or lime.

TEQUILA SOUR

1½ ounces tequila
2½ ounces fresh lemon juice
1 tablespoon superfine sugar
½ slice lemon
maraschino cherry

Shake all ingredients well with ice and strain into a sour glass. Garnish with lemon slice and cherry.

TEQUILA SUNRISE

1½ ounces tequila
4 ounces freshly squeezed orange juice
¾ ounce grenadine

Pour all ingredients, except grenadine, into a mixing glass filled with ice and stir. Strain into a highball glass and add ice cubes. Pour grenadine slowly and allow it to settle to the bottom of the glass.

TEQUILA SUNSET

1½ ounces tequila
1½ ounces fresh lime juice
½ ounce grenadine
1 slice of lime

Put all ingredients into an electric blender. Add one half cup of crushed ice and blend at low speed until smooth. Pour over ice in an old-fashioned glass. Garnish with the slice of lime.

TEQUILA SUNSTROKE

1½ ounces tequila
2 dashes Triple Sec
3 ounces grapefruit juice

Pour ingredients over ice in an old-fashioned glass and stir gently.

TEQUINI

2½ ounces tequila
½ ounce dry vermouth
1 lemon peel

Pour ingredients into a mixing glass filled with ice and stir. Strain into a cocktail glass, twist peel over drink, and drop it into glass.

TOREADOR

1½ ounces tequila
½ ounce white crème de cacao
1 tablespoon heavy cream
whipped cream
cocoa

Shake ingredients thoroughly with ice and strain into a chilled cocktail glass. Garnish with whipped cream and dust it lightly with cocoa.

VIVA VILLA

1½ ounces tequila
2½ ounces lime juice
1 tablespoon superfine sugar

Shake ingredients thoroughly with ice and strain into an ice-filled old-fashioned glass that has been rimmed with salt.

VODKA

The celery rib has now become the accepted garnish for this traditional accompaniment to Sunday brunch: The Bloody Mary.

Rums of Puerto Rico

The Bloody Mary, an ever popular vodka-based cocktail and perhaps the most widely prescribed restorative for the morning after, was invented in Harry's New York Bar in Paris about 1924. Fernand Petiot, the creator of this tomato-juice marvel, originally conceived of it as a short, powerful drink; equal proportions of vodka and tomato juice (two ounces of each), plus a dash of lemon juice, were thoroughly shaken with ice, then strained into a chilled sour glass. Today, some people prefer to add Worcestershire sauce and/or Tabasco, horseradish, celery salt, or lime juice, to the vodka and tomato-juice mixture. Petiot's simple and tasty drink has spawned many variations, with gin, aquavit, tequila, or rum substituted for the vodka.

ADAM'S APPLE

1½ ounces vodka
3 ounces apple cider
1 slice of apple

Pour ingredients over ice into an old-fashioned glass and stir. Garnish with the apple slice.

AQUEDUCT

1½ ounces vodka
1½ teaspoons white curaçao
1½ teaspoons apricot-flavored brandy
1 tablespoon fresh lime juice
1 orange peel

Shake all ingredients well with ice. Strain into a chilled cocktail glass and garnish with the orange peel.

BLACK RUSSIAN

1½ ounces vodka
1½ ounces Kahlúa

Shake ingredients well with ice. Strain into an old-fashioned glass filled with ice.

BLOODY BULL

1½ ounces vodka
3 ounces tomato juice
1½ ounces chilled beef bouillon
1 teaspoon fresh lemon juice
dash salt
dash Worcestershire sauce
dash Tabasco sauce

Shake all ingredients thoroughly with ice. Strain into a sour glass.

BLOODY MARY

1½ ounces vodka
4 ounces tomato juice
1 tablespoon fresh lemon juice
dash Worcestershire sauce
dash Tabasco sauce
salt and freshly ground pepper to taste

Shake all ingredients thoroughly with ice. Strain into a sour glass or into an old-fashioned glass filled with two or three ice cubes. Garnishes may include raw vegetables such as celery, green or red pepper, carrots, zucchini, and cucumber cut into sticks. You may also want to add a cherry tomato or a scallion brush.
  A Danish Mary is made with aquavit instead of vodka; an English Mary is made with gin. A Virgin Mary contains no spirits, which is why some drinkers refer to it as a Bloody Shame.

BLUSHING WOLF

1½ ounces vodka
1 dash grenadine
grapefruit juice

Pour vodka and grenadine over ice in a highball glass. Add grapefruit juice and stir.

BUCKEYE

2¼ ounces vodka
¼ ounce dry vermouth
1 ripe black olive

Pour ingredients into a mixing glass filled with ice and stir until well chilled. Strain into a chilled cocktail glass and garnish with the black olive.

BULLFROG

1½ ounces vodka
4 ounces limeade
1 slice of lime

Pour vodka over ice in a tall glass. Add limeade and stir gently. Garnish with the slice of lime.

BULLSHOT

1½ ounces vodka
4 ounces chilled beef bouillon
salt and freshly ground pepper to taste

Pour ingredients into a mixing glass filled with ice and stir. Strain into a large wineglass or into an old-fashioned glass filled with two or three ice cubes.

CAPE CODDER

1½ ounces vodka
½ ounce fresh lime juice
cranberry juice cocktail
1 slice of orange

Pour ingredients over ice in a highball glass. Stir to mix and garnish with the slice of orange.

CHERRY VODKA

1½ ounces vodka
½ ounce freshly squeezed lime juice
½ ounce Cherry Heering

Shake ingredients thoroughly with ice. Strain into a chilled cocktail glass.

CHOCOLATE RUSSIAN

1½ ounces vodka
1½ ounces Vandermint

Shake ingredients well with ice. Strain into an old-fashioned glass filled with ice.

CINTA

1 ounce vodka
1 ounce brandy
3 dashes Amaretto
maraschino cherry

Pour ingredients into a mixing glass filled with ice and stir. Strain into a chilled cocktail glass and garnish with the cherry.

CLAMDIGGER

1½ ounces vodka
3 ounces bottled clam juice
3 ounces tomato juice
1 dash Tabasco sauce
1 cherry tomato
1 celery rib

Pour ingredients into an ice-filled highball glass and stir. To garnish add the celery rib, and slit the cherry tomato and perch it on the rim of the glass. A convenient shortcut is to substitute 6 ounces of clamato juice.

COPPERHEAD

1 wedge of lime
1½ ounces vodka
ginger ale

Squeeze lime over ice in a highball glass and drop shell into the glass. Pour in vodka, then fill the glass with ginger ale and stir gently.

THE DORCHESTER

1 ounce vodka
1 ounce Campari
chilled brut champagne
1 slice orange

Pour ingredients, except champagne, over ice in a tall glass. Fill the glass with champagne and stir gently. Garnish with the orange slice.

FLYING GRASSHOPPER

1 ounce vodka
½ ounce green crème de menthe
½ ounce white crème de cacao

Pour ingredients into a mixing glass filled with ice and stir well. Strain into a chilled cocktail glass.

FROZEN BIG APPLE

1½ ounces vodka
½ ounce applejack or Calvados
½ ounce fresh lime juice
¼ cup diced apple
½ teaspoon superfine sugar

Put all ingredients into an electric blender. Add one quarter cup of crushed ice and blend at low speed until smooth. Pour into a saucer champagne glass.

GODMOTHER

1½ ounces vodka
¾ ounce Amaretto

Pour ingredients over ice in an old-fashioned glass and stir gently.

GYPSY

2 ounces vodka
½ ounce Benedictine
1 teaspoon fresh lemon juice
1 teaspoon freshly squeezed orange juice
1 slice of orange

Shake ingredients well with ice. Strain over ice into an old-fashioned glass. Garnish with the orange slice.

HARVEY WALLBANGER

1 ounce vodka
4 ounces freshly squeezed orange juice
½ ounce Galliano

Pour vodka and orange juice over ice in a highball glass and stir gently. Float Galliano on top.

MACHETE

1½ ounces vodka
pineapple juice
sparkling mineral water

Pour vodka over ice in a highball glass. Fill glass two thirds full with pineapple juice and top with sparkling mineral water. Stir gently.

MADRAS

1½ ounces vodka
3 ounces cranberry juice cocktail
1½ ounces freshly squeezed orange juice
1 slice of orange

Pour ingredients over ice in a highball glass. Stir to mix and garnish with the slice of orange.

MOSCOW MULE

juice of ½ lime
2 ounces vodka
ginger beer

Squeeze lime over ice in a 12-ounce glass or copper mug and drop into mug. Pour in vodka and fill with ginger beer. Stir gently.

RED APPLE

1 ounce 100-proof vodka
1 ounce apple juice
½ ounce freshly squeezed lemon
 juice
½ teaspoon grenadine
1 dash orange bitters

Shake ingredients well with ice and strain into a chilled cocktail glass.

RITZ BLUE

2¼ ounces vodka
¾ teaspoon dry vermouth
¾ teaspoon blue curaçao
lemon peel

Pour ingredients into a mixing glass filled with ice and stir. Strain into a chilled cocktail glass. Twist peel over drink and drop it into the glass.

RUSSIAN BEAR

1 ounce vodka
½ ounce crème de cacao
½ ounce heavy cream

Shake ingredients vigorously with ice. Strain into a chilled cocktail glass.

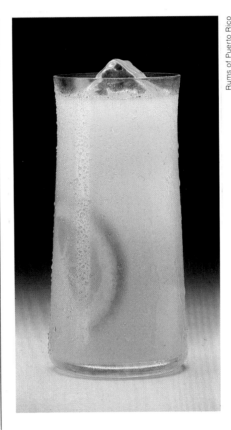

Rums of Puerto Rico

Another brunch favorite, also a wonderfully fragrant summer refresher: the orange juice based Screwdriver (which can also be made with rum or tequila).

SALTY DOG

2 ounces vodka
3 ounces unsweetened grapefruit
 juice
1 teaspoon fresh lemon juice
salt

Shake ingredients thoroughly with ice. Strain into a chilled cocktail glass and sprinkle top of drink with the salt.

SCREWDRIVER

2 ounces vodka
freshly squeezed orange juice
1 slice of orange

Pour vodka over ice in a highball glass. Add orange juice and stir gently.

 A Screwdriver can also be made with rum or tequila.

 For an extra-special brunch treat, float 1 teaspoon of Cointreau on the top of each drink just before serving.

SUNNY SAM

1½ ounces vodka
1½ ounces Sambuca
3 ounces freshly squeezed orange
   juice
1 sprig fresh mint
1 slice of lemon
maraschino cherry

Shake ingredients thoroughly with ice
and strain into an ice-filled old-
fashioned glass. Garnish with the
mint and fruit.

THREE BERRIES

1½ ounces vodka
1 ounce crème de cassis
1 ounce light cream
1 scoop raspberry sherbet
1 fresh strawberry with stem attached
1 sprig fresh mint

Put ingredients into an electric blender
and blend until smooth. Pour into a
wine goblet and garnish with the
strawberry and mint.

TRANSFUSION

1 wedge of lime
1½ ounces vodka
3 ounces unsweetened grape juice
sparkling mineral water or ginger ale

Squeeze lime over ice in a tall glass
and drop it into the glass. Pour in the
grape juice and mixer and stir gently
to mix.

VODKA AND ORANGE FRAPPE

1½ ounces vodka
1 ounce Cointreau
1 ounce light cream
1 scoop orange sherbet
1 slice of orange

Put ingredients into an electric blender
and blend until smooth. Pour into a
chilled wine goblet and garnish with
the orange slice.

VODKA AND TONIC

1 wedge of lime
2 ounces vodka
quinine water

Squeeze lime over ice in a tall glass
and drop the shell into the glass. Pour
in vodka and fill the glass with quinine water. Stir gently.

VODKA COLLINS

2½ ounces vodka
1 or 2 teaspoons superfine sugar
1 ounce fresh lime juice
club soda
1 slice of lemon
1 slice of orange
maraschino cherry

Shake all ingredients except soda
thoroughly with ice. Strain into a
collins glass half filled with ice, and
add club soda. Stir gently. Garnish
with fruit slices and cherry.

VODKA GIBSON

2½ ounces vodka
¼ ounce dry vermouth
1 cocktail onion

Pour vermouth over ice in a mixing
glass. Add vodka and stir gently until
well chilled. Strain into a cocktail
glass and garnish with the onion.

VODKA GIMLET

2½ ounces vodka
½ ounce Rose's lime juice

Pour ingredients into a mixing glass
filled with ice and stir well. Strain into
a chilled cocktail glass.

VODKA HIGHBALL

2 ounces vodka
sparkling mineral water or ginger ale
lemon peel

Pour vodka over ice into a highball
glass, add mixer, and stir gently.
Twist peel over drink and drop into
glass.

VODKA MARTINI

2½ ounces vodka
¼ ounce dry vermouth
1 lemon peel or green olive

Pour ingredients into a mixing glass
filled with ice and stir. Strain into
chilled cocktail glass. Garnish with
the lemon peel or olive. If peel is used,
twist it over drink and drop it into the
glass.

VODKA-ON-THE-ROCKS

2 ounces vodka
1 lemon peel

Pour the vodka over three ice cubes in an old-fashioned glass. Twist peel over drink and drop it into glass.

VODKA RICKEY

juice of half a lime
1½ ounces vodka
sparkling mineral water

Squeeze lime over ice in a tall glass and drop the shell into the glass. Pour in vodka and fill the glass with sparkling mineral water. Stir gently.

VODKA-SAKE MARTINI

2½ ounces vodka
¼ ounce sake
fresh cucumber stick

Pour ingredients into a mixing glass filled with ice and stir. Strain into a chilled cocktail glass or over ice in an old-fashioned glass. Garnish with the cucumber.

VODKA SLING

1 teaspoon superfine sugar
2 tablespoons fresh lemon juice
2 ounces vodka
plain water or sparkling mineral
    water

Stir sugar and lemon juice in a highball glass until sugar dissolves. Fill the glass with ice, add the vodka and mixer, and stir gently.

VODKA SOUR

1½ ounces vodka
2½ ounces fresh lemon juice
1 tablespoon sugar
1 slice of lemon
maraschino cherry

Shake ingredients thoroughly with ice. Strain into a chilled sour glass. Garnish with the lemon slice and cherry. (For a beautiful frothy sour, add 1 tablespoon egg white to other ingredients before shaking.)

VODKA STINGER

1½ ounces vodka
½ ounce white crème de menthe

Shake ingredients vigorously until well chilled. Strain into a chilled cocktail glass.

VOLGA BOATMAN

juice of ½ orange
3 ounces vodka
1 teaspoon kirsch

Shake all ingredients vigorously with ice and strain into a chilled cocktail glass.

WARSAW

1½ ounces vodka
½ ounce blackberry liqueur
½ ounce dry vermouth
1 teaspoon freshly squeezed lemon
    juice
lemon peel

Shake all ingredients well with ice and strain into a chilled cocktail glass. Twist peel over drink and drop it into glass.

WATERMELON COOLER

1½ ounces vodka
½ ounce maraschino
½ ounce fresh lime juice
1 cup fresh watermelon, seeded
1 sprig fresh mint

Put ingredients into an electric blender. Add one half cup crushed ice and blend until smooth. Pour into a tall glass and garnish with the mint.

YELLOW FELLOW

1 ounce vodka
½ ounce Cointreau
2 ounces pineapple juice

Shake ingredients well with ice and strain into a chilled cocktail glass.

YELLOWJACKET

¾ ounce vodka
¾ ounce Benedictine
4 ounces freshly squeezed orange
    juice
½ slice of orange

Shake ingredients well with ice. Strain into a large goblet filled with ice and garnish with the slice of orange.

ZEUS COCKTAIL

2 ounces Campari
1 ounce vodka
lemon peel

Pour ingredients over ice in an old-fashioned glass. Twist peel over drink and drop it into glass.

WHISKEY

Photograph by Don Kushnick

Said to have been named after the Old Manhattan Club in New York City, the marvelous Manhattan, with its smooth taste, is a perennial favorite.

Whiskey covers a lot of ground. Scotland, Ireland, Japan, Canada, and the United States all claim distilleries. Wherever it is made, all whiskey is extracted from grain mash. The proportions of the grains vary, but most whiskies contain a combination of rye, barley, oats, wheat, or corn. America's first well-known distiller of whiskey happened to be a Baptist minister named Elijah Craig. A resident of Kentucky, he baptized his brew bourbon — after a section of the state named in honor of Louis XVI of France (a member of the Bourbon clan). Whiskey, which can be served neat or on the rocks, is also a popular base for many inspired cocktails. Among the classics are the Manhattan, the Mint Julep, and the Rob Roy.

ALGONQUIN

1½ ounces blended whiskey
1 ounce dry vermouth
1 ounce pineapple juice

Shake all ingredients well with ice. Strain into a cocktail glass.

BEALS COCKTAIL

1½ ounces Scotch
½ ounce dry vermouth
½ ounce sweet vermouth

Pour ingredients into a mixing glass filled with ice and stir well. Strain into a chilled cocktail glass.

BLACK HAWK

1¼ ounces blended whiskey
1¼ ounces sloe gin
maraschino cherry

Pour ingredients into a mixing glass filled with ice and stir well. Strain into a chilled cocktail glass and garnish with the cherry.

BLARNEY STONE COCKTAIL

2 ounces Irish whisky
½ teaspoon anisette
½ teaspoon Triple Sec
¼ teaspoon maraschino
1 dash Angostura bitters
1 orange peel
green olive

Shake all ingredients well with ice and strain into a chilled cocktail glass. Twist peel over drink and drop into glass. Garnish with the green olive.

BOILERMAKER

1½ ounces whiskey
ice cold beer or ale

Pour the whiskey into a shot glass and the beer into a chilled mug and serve.

BOURBON HIGHBALL

1½ ounces bourbon
sparkling mineral water or
    plain water
lemon peel (optional)

Pour bourbon over ice cubes in a highball glass. Fill with mixer of choice and stir gently. Twist peel over drink and drop into glass.

BOURBON MANHATTAN

2½ ounces bourbon
½ ounce sweet vermouth
dash Angostura bitters
maraschino cherry

Pour all ingredients into a mixing glass filled with ice and stir. Strain into a cocktail glass and garnish with the cherry.

BOURBONNAISE

1½ ounces bourbon
½ ounce dry vermouth
½ ounce crème de cassis
¼ ounce freshly squeezed lemon
    juice

Shake all ingredients well with ice. Strain into an old-fashioned glass filled with ice.

BOURBON SOUR

1½ ounces bourbon
1½ ounces fresh lemon juice
½ tablespoon superfine sugar
1 slice of lemon
maraschino cherry

Shake all ingredients well with ice. Strain into a chilled sour glass and garnish with the lemon slice and cherry.

CAMERON'S KICK COCKTAIL

¾ ounce Scotch
¾ ounce Irish whisky
1 teaspoon fresh lemon juice
2 dashes orange bitters

Shake ingredients well with ice and strain into a chilled cocktail glass.

CHAPEL HILL

1½ ounces bourbon
½ ounce Triple Sec
1 tablespoon fresh lemon juice
orange peel

Shake ingredients thoroughly with ice and strain into a chilled cocktail glass. Twist orange peel over drink and drop it into the glass.

COMMODORE

1½ ounces blended whiskey
2 teaspoons fresh lime juice
1 teaspoon fresh orange juice
1 teaspoon strawberry liqueur
dash orange bitters
fresh whole strawberry with stem

Shake all ingredients well with ice and strain into a chilled cocktail glass. Garnish with the strawberry.

CREOLE LADY

1½ ounces bourbon
1½ ounces Madeira
1 teaspoon grenadine
green cherry
maraschino cherry

Pour ingredients into a mixing glass filled with ice and stir well. Strain into a chilled cocktail glass and garnish with the cherries.

DELTA

1½ ounces blended whiskey
½ ounce Southern Comfort
½ ounce fresh lime juice
1 slice of orange

Shake all ingredients well with ice and strain into an old-fashioned glass filled with ice. Garnish with orange.

DRY MANHATTAN

2½ ounces blended whiskey
½ ounce dry vermouth
lemon peel or olive

Pour all ingredients into a mixing glass filled with ice and stir. Strain into a chilled cocktail glass. Garnish with lemon twist or olive.

DRY ROB ROY

2½ ounces Scotch
½ ounce dry vermouth
1 lemon peel

Pour all ingredients into a mixing glass filled with ice and stir. Strain into a chilled cocktail glass. Twist peel over drink and drop it into glass.

FINNEGAN'S WAKE

1½ ounces Irish whisky
1½ ounces Irish Mist

Pour ingredients over ice into an old-fashioned glass and stir gently.

GODFATHER

1½ ounces Scotch
¾ ounce Amaretto

Pour ingredients over ice in an old-fashioned glass and stir.

HOLE-IN-ONE COCKTAIL

1¾ ounces Scotch
¾ ounce dry vermouth
¼ teaspoon fresh lemon juice
1 dash orange bitters

Shake all ingredients thoroughly with ice and strain into a chilled cocktail glass.

INCIDER COCKTAIL

1½ ounces blended whiskey
apple cider
slice of apple

Pour ingredients over ice into an old-fashioned glass and stir gently. Garnish with the apple slice.

IRISH RICKEY

wedge of lime
1½ ounces Irish whisky
sparkling mineral water

Squeeze lime over an ice-filled highball glass and drop shell into glass. Add Irish whisky and mixer and stir gently.

JOHN COLLINS

2 ounces blended whiskey
3 ounces lemon juice
1 or 2 teaspoons superfine sugar
club soda or sparkling mineral water
1 slice each of lemon and orange
maraschino cherry

Shake well all ingredients, except mixer, with ice. Strain into a collins glass filled with ice and garnish with the fruit.

KENTUCKY COCKTAIL

1½ ounces bourbon
¾ ounce pineapple juice

Shake ingredients thoroughly with ice and strain into a chilled cocktail glass.

KENTUCKY COLONEL

½ ounce Benedictine
1½ ounces bourbon
lemon peel

Pour ingredients into a mixing glass filled with ice and strain into a chilled cocktail glass. Twist lemon peel over drink and drop it into the glass.

MANHATTAN

2½ ounces blended whiskey
½ ounce sweet vermouth
dash Angostura bitters
maraschino cherry

Pour all ingredients into a mixing glass filled with ice and stir. Strain into a cocktail glass and garnish with the cherry.

The Mint Julep—traditionally served in a silver cup garnished with fresh mint—is a symbol of Southern hospitality, and the centerpiece of Kentucky Derby Day festivities across the nation.

MINT JULEP

4 sprigs fresh mint
1 teaspoon superfine sugar
3 ounces bourbon

Fill a tall glass or silver tumbler with crushed ice. In a small glass, muddle the leaves from two mint sprigs with sugar and a splash of water. Add bourbon, stir gently, and strain into the tall glass. Garnish with the remaining mint sprigs.

MORNING GLORY

1½ ounces fresh lemon juice
1 teaspoon superfine sugar
2½ ounces Scotch
6 drops Pernod
½ egg white
2 teaspoons heavy cream

Shake ingredients vigorously with ice and strain into a chilled wine glass.

NEW YORKER

1½ ounces blended whiskey
½ ounce fresh lime juice
1 teaspoon superfine sugar
¼ teaspoon grenadine
1 peel each of lemon and orange

Shake all ingredients well with ice. Strain into a sugar-frosted cocktail glass. Twist peels over drink and drop them into the glass.

NIGHT SHADE

1½ ounces bourbon
½ ounce sweet vermouth
1 ounce freshly squeezed orange juice
¼ teaspoon yellow Chartreuse
½ slice each of lemon and orange

Shake all ingredients well with ice. Strain into an old-fashioned glass filled with ice. Garnish with the fruit.

OLD-FASHIONED

½ teaspoon superfine sugar
2 dashes Angostura bitters
1 teaspoon water
2 ounces blended whiskey
1 lemon peel
1 orange slice (optional)
maraschino cherry (optional)

Stir sugar, bitters, and water in an old-fashioned glass until sugar dissolves. Fill the glass with ice, add the whiskey, and stir well. Twist peel over drink and drop it into glass. Garnish with orange and cherry.

PADDY COCKTAIL

1½ ounces Irish whisky
1½ ounces sweet vermouth
1 dash Angostura bitters

Pour ingredients into a mixing glass filled with ice and strain into a chilled cocktail glass.

PERFECT MANHATTAN

1½ ounces blended whiskey
¼ ounce sweet vermouth
¼ ounce dry vermouth
dash Angostura bitters
maraschino cherry

Pour all ingredients into a mixing glass filled with ice and stir. Strain into a cocktail glass and garnish.

PERFECT ROB ROY

1½ ounces Scotch
¼ ounce sweet vermouth
¼ ounce dry vermouth
dash Angostura bitters
maraschino cherry

Pour all ingredients into a mixing glass filled with ice and stir. Strain into a cocktail glass and garnish.

PRESBYTERIAN

3 ounces bourbon
2 ounces ginger ale
2 ounces club soda
1 lemon peel

Pour bourbon into an ice-filled highball glass and add mixers. Stir gently. Twist peel over drink and drop it into the glass.

PRINCE EDWARD

1½ ounces Scotch
½ ounce Lillet
¼ ounce Drambuie
1 slice of orange

Shake all ingredients well with ice. Strain into an old-fashioned glass filled with ice. Garnish with the orange slice.

ROB ROY

2½ ounces Scotch
½ ounce sweet vermouth
maraschino cherry

Pour all ingredients into a mixing glass filled with ice and stir. Strain into a cocktail glass and garnish with the cherry.

SAZERAC

1 ounce Pernod
½ teaspoon superfine sugar
¼ teaspoon Peychaud's bitters
2 ounces bourbon or rye whiskey
1 lemon peel
Swirl Pernod around in a prechilled old-fashioned glass until the inside is completely coated. Discard excess. Pour remaining ingredients into a mixing glass filled with ice and stir until sugar is dissolved. Strain into the coated glass. Twist peel over drink and drop it into the glass.

SCOTCH HIGHBALL

1½ ounces Scotch
plain water or sparkling mineral
    water
1 lemon peel (optional)

Pour Scotch over ice cubes in a highball glass. Fill with mixer and stir gently. Twist peel over drink and drop it into glass.

SCOTCH MILK PUNCH

2 ounces Scotch
6 ounces chilled whole milk
½ teaspoon superfine sugar
freshly grated nutmeg

Shake all ingredients well with ice. Strain into a chilled wine goblet and dust with nutmeg.

SCOTCH MINT COOLER

2 ounces Scotch
3 dashes white crème de menthe
club soda or sparkling mineral water

Pour ingredients, except mixer, into a highball glass filled with ice. Fill with mixer and stir gently.

SCOTCH MIST

2 ounces Scotch
lemon twist
straw

Pack an old-fashioned glass with crushed ice and add Scotch. Garnish with a lemon twist and serve with a straw.

SCOTCH SOUR

2 ounces Scotch
2 tablespoons fresh lemon juice
1 teaspoon superfine sugar
1 slice of orange
maraschino cherry

Shake all ingredients well with ice and strain into a sour glass. Garnish with the orange slice and cherry.

SEABOARD

1 ounce blended whiskey
1 ounce gin
1 ounce fresh lemon juice
1 teaspoon superfine sugar
2 sprigs fresh mint

Shake all ingredients well with ice. Strain into an old-fashioned glass filled with ice. Garnish with the mint.

SINGAPORE

1½ ounces Canadian whiskey
¼ ounce sloe gin
¼ ounce Rose's lime juice
½ ounce fresh lemon juice
cucumber peel

Shake all ingredients well with ice. Strain into an old-fashioned glass filled with ice. Garnish with peel.

SOUTHERN SOUR

1 ounce bourbon
1 ounce Southern Comfort
2 tablespoons fresh lemon juice
1 teaspoon superfine sugar
1 slice of orange
maraschino cherry

Shake all ingredients well with ice and strain into a sour glass. Garnish with the orange slice and cherry.

THUNDERCLAP COCKTAIL

¾ ounce blended whiskey
¾ ounce gin
¾ ounce brandy

Shake ingredients well with ice and strain into a chilled cocktail glass.

T.N.T. COCKTAIL

1½ ounces blended whiskey
1½ ounces anisette

Shake ingredients well with ice and strain into a chilled cocktail glass.

TROIS RIVIÈRES

1½ ounces Canadian whisky
1 ounce Dubonnet
½ ounce Triple Sec
orange peel

Shake ingredients well with ice and strain over ice into an old-fashioned glass. Twist orange peel over drink and drop it into glass.

TWIN HILLS

1½ ounces blended whiskey
2 teaspoons Benedictine
1½ teaspoons fresh lemon juice
1½ teaspoons fresh lime juice
1 teaspoon superfine sugar
1 slice each of lemon and lime

Shake ingredients thoroughly with ice and strain into a chilled sour glass. Garnish with the fruit slices.

WARD EIGHT

2 ounces blended whiskey
½ ounce fresh lemon juice
1 teaspoon superfine sugar
½ teaspoon grenadine
1 slice of lemon

Shake all ingredients well with ice. Strain into a tall glass filled with ice and garnish with the lemon slice.

WHISKEY HIGHBALL

1½ ounces whiskey
plain water or sparkling mineral
   water
1 lemon peel (optional)

Pour whiskey over ice cubes in a highball glass. Fill with mixer and stir gently. Twist peel over drink and drop it into glass.

WHISKEY MILK PUNCH

2 ounces whiskey of choice
6 ounces chilled whole milk
½ teaspoon superfine sugar
freshly grated nutmeg

Shake all ingredients well with ice. Strain into a chilled wine goblet and dust with nutmeg.

WHISKEY SOUR

2 ounces blended whiskey
2½ ounces fresh lemon juice
1 tablespoon superfine sugar
1 slice of orange
maraschino cherry

Shake all ingredients well with ice and strain into a sour glass. Garnish with the orange slice and cherry.

AFTER-DINNER
AND
CREAM DRINKS

Photograph by Don Kushnick

Rich and vibrant, the many hues of cordials and liqueurs are pleasing to the eye and delightful to the palate.

After-dinner and cream drinks are usually served, sipped, and savored away from the dining-room table. Some of your guests may request their favorite liqueur or brandy served neat, while others may prefer a more dessertlike and creamy beverage. Mists and frappes are a change of pace, and if you want to show off your skills as a mixologist, carefully pour the rainbow cordial known as a Pousse-café.

A AND B

½ ounce Benedictine
½ ounce applejack

Carefully pour the ingredients in the order listed into a straight-sided liqueur glass, so that the applejack floats on top of the Benedictine.

ALFONSO

2 ounces crème de cacao
½ ounce heavy cream

Pour crème de cacao into a large liqueur glass and carefully float the cream on top.

AMARETTO AND CREAM

1½ ounces Amaretto
1½ ounces heavy cream

Shake ingredients vigorously with ice and strain into a chilled cocktail glass.

AMARETTO STINGER

1½ ounces Amaretto
¾ ounce white crème de menthe

Shake ingredients well with ice and strain into a chilled cocktail glass.

ANGEL'S DELIGHT

¼ ounce grenadine
¼ ounce Triple Sec
¼ ounce Crème Yvette
¼ ounce heavy cream

Pour ingredients in the order listed into a pousse-café or straight-sided liqueur glass. Pour carefully so that each ingredient floats on top of the one beneath it.

ANGEL'S KISS

¼ ounce crème de cacao
¼ ounce Crème Yvette
¼ ounce heavy cream

Pour ingredients in the order listed into a pousse-café or straight-sided liqueur glass. Pour carefully so that each ingredient floats on top of the one beneath it.

ANGEL'S WING

½ ounce crème de cacao
½ ounce brandy
1 tablespoon heavy cream

Pour ingredients in the order listed into a pousse-café or straight-sided liqueur glass. Pour carefully so that each ingredient floats on top of the one beneath it.

BETWEEN THE SHEETS

¾ ounce light rum
¾ ounce brandy
¾ ounce Cointreau
½ ounce fresh lemon juice

Shake ingredients well with ice and strain into a chilled cocktail glass.

BRANDY MIST

2½ ounces Metaxa

Pack an old-fashioned glass with half a cup of crushed ice. Pour brandy over it, and serve with a straw.

CADIZ

¾ ounce dry sherry
¾ ounce blackberry liqueur
½ ounce Triple Sec
½ ounce heavy cream

Shake ingredients vigorously with ice. Strain into a chilled old-fashioned glass.

CARA SPOUSA

1 ounce coffee liqueur
1 ounce white curaçao
½ ounce heavy cream

Put all ingredients into an electric blender or food processor. Add one third cup of crushed ice and blend at low speed until smooth. Pour into a saucer champagne glass.

CHERRY RUM

1¼ ounces light rum
¾ ounce cherry liqueur
½ ounce heavy cream

Put all ingredients into an electric blender. Add one third cup crushed ice and blend at low speed until smooth. Pour into a chilled saucer champagne glass.

CHOCOLATE MINT CREAM

1½ ounces Vandermint
1½ ounces light cream

Shake ingredients well with ice and pour over ice in an old-fashioned glass.

CHOCOLATE RUM

1 ounce light rum
½ ounce crème de cacao
½ ounce white crème de menthe
½ ounce heavy cream
1 teaspoon 151-proof rum

Shake all ingredients, except 151-proof rum, thoroughly with ice. Strain into a chilled cocktail glass and carefully float the rum on top.

COFFEE AND ORANGE FRAPPE

½ ounce coffee liqueur
½ ounce Grand Marnier
½ ounce freshly squeezed orange juice
1 slice of orange

Stir ingredients well without ice. Pour over a half cup of crushed ice packed into a saucer champagne glass. Garnish with the orange slice.

COFFEE GRASSHOPPER

¾ ounce coffee liqueur
¾ ounce white crème de menthe
1 ounce heavy cream

Shake ingredients vigorously with ice and strain into a chilled cocktail glass.

CRÈME DE MENTHE FRAPPE

2 ounces green crème de menthe

Pack a saucer champagne glass with finely crushed ice. Pour crème de menthe over ice and serve with a short straw.

FIFTH AVENUE

½ ounce crème de cacao
½ ounce apricot-flavored brandy
1 tablespoon heavy cream

Pour ingredients in the order listed into a straight-sided liqueur glass. Pour carefully so that each ingredient floats on top of the one beneath it.

GOLDEN CADILLAC

¾ ounce crème de cacao
¾ ounce Galliano
¾ ounce heavy cream

Put all ingredients into an electric blender. Add one third cup of crushed ice and blend at low speed until smooth. Pour into a saucer champagne glass.

GOLDEN DREAM

1 ounce Galliano
½ ounce Triple Sec
1 ounce freshly squeezed orange juice
1 ounce heavy cream

Shake all ingredients thoroughly with ice and strain into a chilled cocktail glass.

GOLDEN GOPHER

1½ ounces white crème de cacao
1½ ounces brandy

Pour ingredients into a mixing glass filled with ice and stir. Strain into a chilled cocktail glass.

GRASSHOPPER

¾ ounce crème de cacao
¾ ounce crème de menthe
¾ ounce heavy cream

Shake ingredients vigorously with ice and strain into a chilled cocktail glass.

GREEN DRAGON

1 ounce green crème de menthe
1½ ounces vodka

Stir ingredients well without ice. Pour over a half cup of crushed ice packed into a saucer champagne glass.

ITALIAN SOMBRERO

1½ ounces Amaretto
3 ounces heavy cream

Shake ingredients vigorously with ice. Strain into a chilled cocktail glass or over ice into an old-fashioned glass.

JAMAICA HOP

1 ounce coffee-flavored brandy
1 ounce white crème de cacao
1 ounce light cream

Shake ingredients vigorously with ice and strain into a chilled cocktail glass.

KAHLÚA TOREADOR

1 ounce Kahlúa
2 ounces brandy
1 egg white

Shake all ingredients vigorously with ice and strain into a chilled cocktail glass.

LA DOLCE MARIA

1 ounce Amaretto
1 ounce heavy cream
1 ounce vodka

Shake ingredients vigorously with ice. Strain into a chilled saucer champagne glass.

MELON POUSSE-CAFÉ

½ ounce Crème de noyau
½ ounce white crème de cacao
½ ounce Midori

Pour ingredients in the order listed into a pousse-café or straight-sided liqueur glass. Pour carefully so that each ingredient floats on top of the one beneath it.

MOCHA MINT

¾ ounce coffee liqueur
¾ ounce white crème de menthe
¾ ounce white crème de cacao

Shake ingredients thoroughly with ice. Strain into a chilled, sugar-frosted cocktail glass.

MOONGLOW

1 ounce white crème de cacao
1 ounce Benedictine
1 ounce light cream

Shake ingredients vigorously with ice and strain into a small, chilled wineglass.

PERNOD FRAPPE

1½ ounces Pernod
½ ounce anisette
2 dashes Angostura bitters

Stir ingredients well without ice. Pour over a half cup of crushed ice packed into a saucer champagne glass.

PINK LADY

1 egg white
1 teaspoon grenadine
1 teaspoon heavy cream
1½ ounces gin

Shake ingredients vigorously with ice and strain into a chilled cocktail glass.

PINK SQUIRREL

1 ounce Crème de noyau
1 ounce white crème de cacao
¾ ounce heavy cream

Shake ingredients vigorously with ice. Strain into a chilled, sugar-frosted cocktail glass.

POUSSE-CAFÉ

1 teaspoon grenadine
1 teaspoon yellow Chartreuse
1 teaspoon Crème Yvette
1 teaspoon white crème de menthe
1 teaspoon green Chartreuse
1 teaspoon brandy

Pour ingredients in the order listed into a pousse-café or straight-sided liqueur glass. Pour carefully so that each ingredient floats on top of the one beneath it.

PRINCESS

2 ounces apricot brandy
½ ounce heavy cream

Pour apricot brandy into a large liqueur glass and carefully float the cream on top.

RUM FRAPPE

1 scoop pineapple sherbet
2 ounces light rum
1 pineapple stick

Put all ingredients into an electric blender and blend at low speed until smooth. Pour into a saucer champagne glass and garnish with the pineapple stick.
Other variations of this drink can be made by substituting lime sherbet, orange sherbet, or lemon sherbet. Appropriate garnishes would be slices of fresh fruit and grated peels.

RUM MIST

1½ ounces light rum
1 teaspoon 151-proof rum
1 slice of lime

Pack an old-fashioned glass with half a cup of crushed ice. Pour the light rum over it, then carefully float the 151-proof rum on top. Garnish with the slice of lime and serve with a straw.

RUSSIAN COFFEE

¾ ounce coffee liqueur
¾ ounce vodka
¾ ounce heavy cream

Put all ingredients into an electric blender. Add one third cup of crushed ice and blend at low speed until smooth. Pour into a saucer champagne glass.

RUSTY NAIL

1½ ounces Scotch
1½ ounces Drambuie

Pour ingredients over ice into a chilled old-fashioned glass. Stir gently.

SAMBUCA CON TRES MOSCI

1½ ounces Sambuca
3 roasted coffee beans

Warm the Sambuca and pour it into a liqueur glass. Add the coffee beans and light the Sambuca just before serving.

SARONNO

1 ounce brandy
1 ounce Amaretto
1 ounce heavy cream

Shake all ingredients vigorously with ice. Strain into a chilled cocktail glass.

SCOTCH MIST

1½ ounces heavy, full-bodied Scotch

Pack an old-fashioned glass with half a cup of crushed ice. Pour Scotch over it and serve with a straw.

SLOE LIME FRAPPE

1 ounce sloe gin
½ ounce light rum
1 slice of lime

Stir ingredients well without ice. Pour over crushed ice in a saucer champagne glass. Garnish with the lime slice.

SOMBRERO

1½ ounces Kahlúa
1 ounce heavy cream

Pour the Kahlúa into a large liqueur glass and carefully float the cream on top.

ZORBA

1½ ounces Metaxa
¾ ounce Amaretto

Pour ingredients over ice in an old-fashioned glass.

These delicious Rum Frappes are made with lime and pineapple sherbet. They are attractive and easy ways to present dessert in a glass.

Photograph by Don Kushnick

COFFEE DRINKS

Mocha Rum, garnished with whipped cream.

A strong, well-brewed cup of black coffee is welcome at the close of any meal. But if served piping hot and laced with brandy, spirits, or liqueur it adds a particularly special finishing touch. The coffee's heat releases the flavor and bouquet of any added spirit. The liqueurs that taste best when mixed with coffee are Amaretto, Galliano, Benedictine, Drambuie, Strega, and anisette. Brandy, Cognac, and Armagnac are also pleasing. A hot drink such as Irish Coffee can be savored on a cold, wintry afternoon, and a cold version of it is wonderfully refreshing after a meal served on a hot summer day. Spectacular coffee presentations for after-dinner sipping include Café Brûlot, its cousin Café Diable, and Café Royale.

AMARETTO CAFÉ

1 ounce Amaretto
4 ounces hot, strong coffee

Pour Amaretto and coffee into a demitasse cup and stir gently.

CAFÉ AU KIRSCH

1 ounce kirsch
1 ounce cold, strong black coffee
½ teaspoon superfine sugar
1 egg white

Put ingredients into an electric blender. Add one cup of cracked ice and blend at high speed until thick and smooth. Pour, unstrained, into a chilled cocktail glass. Present the drink with a straw.

CAFÉ BRÛLOT

6 lumps sugar
9 ounces brandy
1 lemon peel
2 orange peels
2 cinnamon sticks, broken in half
6 whole cloves
1½ cups strong, hot coffee

Put all ingredients, except coffee, into a chafing dish or into an attractive saucepan over a warmer. Heat slowly until warm, then light the mixture and let it flame for about a minute. Slowly pour in the coffee, stir gently, and ladle into 6 demitasse cups.

CAFÉ CACAO FRAPPE

2 ounces cold, strong black coffee
2 ounces crème de cacao
superfine sugar

Sweeten coffee to taste. Pour ingredients into a shaker and add one half cup of crushed ice. Shake vigorously and pour, unstrained, into a chilled saucer champagne glass. Present the drink with a straw.

CAFÉ CHARENTAIS

4 ounces hot, strong coffee
sugar
1 ounce brandy
1 tablespoon whipped cream

Pour the coffee into a demitasse cup, sweeten it to taste, add the brandy, and stir gently. Top with whipped cream.

CAFÉ DIABLE

2 cinnamon sticks, broken in half
2 tablespoons superfine sugar
½ cup dark Jamaican rum
zest of 2 oranges stuck with 18 whole
    cloves
6 cups strong, hot coffee

Put all ingredients, except coffee, into a chafing dish or into an attractive saucepan over a warmer. Heat slowly until warm, then light the mixture and let it flame for about a minute. Slowly pour in the coffee, stir gently, and ladle into 6 large coffee cups or mugs.

CAFÉ PUCCI

1 ounce golden rum
1 ounce Amaretto
5 ounces strong, hot coffee
1 tablespoon whipped cream

Pour rum and Amaretto into an 8-ounce mug and add hot coffee. Stir gently. Top with whipped cream.

CAFÉ ROMANO

1 ounce Sambuca
4 ounces hot, strong coffee

Pour Sambuca and coffee into a demitasse cup and stir gently.

CAFÉ ROYALE

1 sugar cube
1 tablespoon brandy
4 ounces hot, strong coffee

Soak the sugar cube in the brandy in a teaspoon and hold it so that it rests on top of a demitasse cup full of coffee. Ignite the cube and when the flame dies, drop the contents of the spoon into the cup and stir.

CAFÉ ROYALE FRAPPE

2 ounces cold, strong black coffee
1 ounce brandy
superfine sugar

Sweeten coffee to taste. Pour ingredients into a shaker and add one half cup crushed ice. Shake vigorously and pour, unstrained, into a chilled saucer champagne glass. Present the drink with a straw.

COFFEE COCKTAIL

1½ ounces brandy
½ ounce Cointreau
1½ ounces strong, chilled black
   coffee

Shake ingredients thoroughly with ice
and strain into a chilled cocktail glass.

COFFEE WITH COGNAC

1 lemon peel
superfine sugar
4 ounces strong, hot coffee
1 ounce cognac

Rub the rim of a demitasse cup with
the lemon peel and frost with sugar.
Fill the cup with hot coffee and carefully float the brandy on top. Light
the brandy and serve.

COLD COFFEE FRAPPE

4 ounces strong, chilled black coffee
4 ounces French vanilla ice cream
1½ ounces brandy

Put ingredients into an electric blender
and blend until smooth. Pour into a
large wineglass or goblet.

DUTCH COFFEE

2 ounces Vandermint
5 ounces hot, strong coffee
1 tablespoon whipped cream
cocoa

Pour ingredients into a coffee mug
and stir gently. Top with whipped
cream and dust lightly with cocoa.

GRAND COFFEE

sugar to taste
6 ounces hot, strong coffee
2 tablespoons Grand Marnier
1 tablespoon whipped cream
freshly grated orange rind

Pour coffee into a mug, and add sugar
to taste. Add Grand Marnier, and stir
gently. Top with whipped cream and
sprinkle freshly grated orange rind on
top.

ICED COFFEE

8 ounces chilled, strong coffee
½ ounce Tia Maria (or to taste)
light cream (optional)

Pour coffee over ice in a tall glass, add
Tia Maria and cream, and stir gently.

IRISH COFFEE

1 teaspoon superfine sugar
1½ ounces Irish whiskey or Irish Mist
5 ounces hot, strong coffee
1 tablespoon whipped cream or
   1 tablespoon heavy cream

Put all ingredients, except cream, into
a warmed, stemmed 8-ounce goblet
and stir until the sugar is dissolved.
Top with whipped cream or float the
heavy cream on top.

JAMAICAN COFFEE

1 ounce Tia Maria
¾ ounce light rum
5 ounces hot, strong coffee
1 tablespoon whipped cream
freshly grated nutmeg

Put all ingredients, except cream, into
a warmed, stemmed 8-ounce goblet
and stir gently. Top with whipped
cream and dust lightly with nutmeg.

KAHLÚA COFFEE

1½ ounces Kahlúa
5 ounces hot, strong coffee
1 tablespoon whipped cream
ground cinnamon

Pour all ingredients, except cream,
into a warmed, stemmed 8-ounce
goblet and stir gently. Top with
whipped cream and dust lightly with
ground cinnamon.

MEXICAN COFFEE

¾ ounce brandy
¾ ounce Kahlúa
5 ounces hot, strong coffee
1 tablespoon whipped cream

Pour all ingredients, except cream,
into a warmed, stemmed 8-ounce
goblet and stir gently. Top with
whipped cream.

MOCHA RUM

1½ ounces rum
3 ounces strong, hot coffee
3 ounces hot cocoa
superfine sugar
whipped cream

Pour rum, coffee, and cocoa into a
glass mug, add superfine sugar to taste,
stir until sugar is dissolved and garnish with the whipped cream.

VESUVIO

¾ ounce Sambuca
1 cup hot, strong coffee
1 sugar cube

Float half of the Sambuca on the coffee. Place the sugar cube in a dessert
spoon and add the rest of the Sambuca. Light with a match and dip the
spoon into the coffee cup. Stir.

DICK TAEUBER'S CORDIAL PIE

Mr. Dick Taeuber, inspired by a recipe for a Brandy Alexander pie that had appeared in *The New York Times*, retreated to his kitchen and created the following variations on the theme. He also included the information that "the pie freezes, or more important, thaws, quite well, which means that it can be made further in advance of use than the night before, as has been the custom in my home."

1½ cups crumbs
  (graham crackers,
  chocolate wafers, or
  gingersnaps)
¼ cup melted butter
  (⅓ cup with graham-
  cracker crumbs)
½ cup cold water
1 envelope unflavored
  gelatin

⅔ cup sugar
⅛ teaspoon salt
3 eggs, separated
½ cup of liqueurs or liquor,
  as directed on chart
1 cup heavy cream
  Food coloring

1. Preheat oven to 350 degrees.
2. Combine crumbs with butter. Form in a 9-inch pan and bake for 10 minutes. Cool.
3. Pour the water in a saucepan and sprinkle gelatin over it. Add ⅓ cup sugar, salt, and egg yolks. Stir to blend.
4. Place over low heat and stir until gelatin dissolves and mixture thickens. DO NOT BOIL! Remove from heat.
5. Stir the liqueurs or liquor into the mixture. Then chill until mixture starts to mound slightly.
6. Beat egg whites until stiff, then add remaining sugar and beat until peaks are firm. Fold meringue into thickened mixture.
7. Whip the cream, then fold into mixture. Add food coloring if desired.
8. Turn mixture into crust. Add garnish, if desired. Chill several hours or overnight.
Yield: 6 servings

OPTIONS

	Liquors (Equal parts, ½ cup total)	Crust (Graham can be used for any)	Garnish
1. Brandy Alexander	Cognac, brown crème de cacao	Graham cracker	Chocolate curls
2. Chocolate mint	White crème de menthe, brown crème de cacao	Chocolate cooky	Chocolate curls
3. Grasshopper	White crème de menthe, green crème de menthe	Chocolate cooky	
4. Eggnog	Rum	Gingersnap	Nutmeg
5. Banana mint	Crème de banana, white crème de menthe	Graham cracker	
6. Pink squirrel	Crème d'almond, white crème de cacao	Graham cracker	
7. Brown velvet	Triple sec, brown crème de cacao	Chocolate cooky	
8. Irish coffee	Irish whisky (use double strength coffee in place of water)	Graham cracker	
9. Golden dream	Galliano, Cointreau (use ¾ cup of orange juice in place of water, add 2 tablespoons grated orange peel)	Graham cracker	Toasted coconut
10. Midnight cowboy	Chocolate mint, brandy	Chocolate cooky	
11. Italian mousse	Chocolate mint, vodka	Chocolate cooky	
12. Fifth Avenue	Apricot brandy, brown crème de cacao	Chocolate cooky	
13. Raspberry Alexander	3 ounces raspberry brandy, 1 ounce white crème de cacao	Graham cracker	
14. Blackberry Alexander	3 ounces blackberry brandy, 1 ounce white crème de cacao	Chocolate cooky	

	Liquors (Equal parts, ½ cup total)	Crust (Graham can be used for any)	Garnish
15. Banana chocolate cream	Crème de banana, white crème de cacao	Chocolate cooky	
16. George Washington	Chocolate mint, cherry brandy	Chocolate cooky	
17. Shady lady	Coffee-flavored brandy, triple sec (use coffee in place of water)	Chocolate cooky	
18. Cheri Suisse	Cherry Suisse (cherry chocolate)	Chocolate cooky	
19. Vandermint	Vandermint (chocolate mint)	Chocolate cooky	
20. Sabra	Sabra (orange chocolate)	Chocolate cooky	

PICK-ME-UPS

Pick-me-ups may not be what the *doctor* ordered for a bad "morning after," but they can be just what *you* need to get going again. Some people recommend the "hair of the dog," while others swear by the Bloody Mary or the Prairie Oyster. But most people agree that the best remedy is just a matter of time.

CHAMPAGNE PICK-ME-UP

1½ ounces brandy
3 dashes curaçao
3 dashes Fernet-Branca
4 ounces chilled brut champagne

Pour all ingredients, except champagne, into a tall glass over three ice cubes and stir to mix. Pour in the champagne and stir gently.

CLAM JUICE COCKTAIL

4 ounces bottled clam juice
1 tablespoon ketchup
1½ teaspoons fresh lemon juice
1 dash Worcestershire sauce
salt and pepper to taste
celery salt

Shake ingredients thoroughly with ice and strain into a large, chilled wineglass. Dust lightly with celery salt.

EYE OPENER

2 ounces light rum
1 teaspoon crème de cacao
1 teaspoon Pernod
1 egg yolk

Shake all ingredients vigorously with ice. Strain into a chilled cocktail glass.

PRAIRIE OYSTER

1 egg yolk
1 teaspoon Worcestershire sauce
2 dashes vinegar
1 dash Tabasco sauce
salt and pepper to taste

Slide the egg yolk into a large wineglass and add the remaining ingredients. Swirl glass gently to blend ingredients without breaking the yolk. Swallow the egg yolk whole.

RED BIRD

1 ounce vodka
3 ounces tomato juice
ice-cold beer

Pour ingredients, except beer, over ice into a tall glass. Add beer and stir gently.

SHERRY AND EGG

1 whole egg
2½ ounces sherry

Crack the egg and put it into a cocktail glass. Add the sherry and drink quickly.

BUYING GUIDE FOR PARTIES

Use the following chart as a guideline for stocking your party bar. To be absolutely sure that you have plenty of supplies on hand, substitute quart or liter-size bottles for fifths. The calculations for wine are based on serving a single red or white wine throughout the meal. When purchasing club soda, sparkling mineral water, ginger ale, or quinine water, allow a quart-size bottle for three persons.

COCKTAILS

Number of guests	Number of 1½ ounce drinks	Have on hand
6	12-18	2 fifths
8	16-24	2 fifths
12	24-36	3 fifths
20	40-60	5 fifths

WINE AND CHAMPAGNE

Number of guests	Number of 4 ounce servings	Have on hand
6	12	2 fifths
8	16	3 fifths
12	24	4 fifths
20	40	7 fifths

BRANDY AND LIQUEURS

Number of guests	Number of 1 or 1½ ounce servings	Have on hand
6	6-12	1 fifth
8	8-16	1 fifth
12	12-24	1 fifth
20	20-40	2 fifths

ACKNOWLEDGMENTS

We are grateful to the following individuals and corporations for information and material which they were good enough to provide for this volume.

Letitia Baldrige Enterprises; The Boulders Inn of New Preston, Connecticut; The Canada Dry Corporation; Sally Stroker at Grey Advertising; Salla Kajanne at IITTALA GLASSWORKS; Sydney J. Cohn and Lee Cardaci at Pesin, Sydney & Bernard Advertising; Marcia Bain at Ruder & Finn; Kristin Hubbard at Rums of Puerto Rico; Annette Perlman at Joseph E. Seagram & Sons, Inc.; and Mrs. Sylvia Dowling and Mr. Henry Zbrkiewicz at The "21" Club.

INDEX